WHAT THE ANCIENT AFRICAN KNEW

and how their works influenced modern life

Yemi Adesina

ISBN: 979-8-35520-200-2

CONTENTS

APOLOGIA. 7

THE AUTHOR 9

ACKNOWLEDGEMENTS 11

1. INTRODUCTION 13

2. WHY TEACH AFRICAN HISTORY 21

3. THE IMPACT OF AFRICA'S GEOGRAPHY ON AFRICAN DEVELOPMENT. 27

4. THE BASICS OF AFRICAN HISTORY. 43

5. HOW AGRICULTURE BEGAN IN AFRICA 57

6. WHAT THE ANCIENT AFRICAN KNEW ABOUT MANUFACTURING. 63

    Calendar. 64

    Astronomy 66

    Abstract art. 67

    Mathematics 68

    Algorithms. 69

    Paper 71

    Written language 72

    Educational Institutions 73

    Medicine 75

    Steel 77

    Glass. 79

    Architecture 81

    Mobile phones. 82

    Cotton 83

    Limitations of African manufacturing 84

7. WHAT THE AFRICAN ANCIENTS KNEW ABOUT FOOD MANUFACTURING........87

Kola Nut..88

Palm oil..89

Coffee...90

Shea butter...92

African Rice..93

Yam..95

Sorghum..97

Other crops..99

Jollof rice...100

8. INTERNATIONAL TRADE IN ANCIENT AFRICA BEFORE SLAVERY.............103

The Egyptian Empire...104

The kingdom of Axum was around Ethiopia...........................106

The kingdom of Nubia..107

Benin Empire and the Great Walls of Benin.........................108

The Asante kingdom..113

The Anglo-Asante Wars...114

Yaa Asantewaa and the War of the Golden Stool.....................115

Mali Empire...116

The astronomical knowledge of the Dogon tribe of Mali dates back to 3200 BC........118

Kingdom of Zimbabwe (1220-1450 AD)................................119

Oyo Empire..120

9. THE AFRICAN DIASPORA CONTRIBUTION TO MODERN CIVILISATION........125

10. IS SUBSTANCE MISUSE TO BLAME FOR AFRICAN UNDERDEVELOPMENT?...131

11. THE IMPACT OF SLAVERY ON AFRICA.....................................135

12. HOW AFRICANS AIDED THE INDUSTRIAL AGE..............................145

13. HOW THE COLONIALISATION OF AFRICA EXPANDED THE EUROPE'S INFLUENCE...153

14. THE CONSEQUENCES OF THE COLONISATION OF AFRICAN COUNTRIES.....163

15. AFRICA AT INDEPENDENCE...165
    Internal Factors..167
    External factors 168
    Military interventions 170

16. THE FUTURE OF AFRICA 171
    Let us get the basics right first..172

17. GLOSSARY AND TERMS...187

18. REFERENCES 193

This page intentionally left blank

APOLOGIA

There are bound to be — only a few, I hope — errors and omissions, and I apologise in advance. No man knows it all, especially me! And you learn more as you get older. With age, one good thing is that you are happy to confess you don't know and are content to pass the inquiry on to a specialist who probably does.

This book is dedicated to hardworking, patient, enthusiastic, generally under-rewarded, and underappreciated farmers of Africa, some of whom I've met, worked with and always listened to — all of whom have contributed to food production in Africa.

This page intentionally left blank

The Author

Mr Yemi Adesina is the founder of Boyd Agro-Allied Ltd, one of the largest pig farms in Nigeria. He is also the CEO of Pristine Integrated Farm Resources Ltd, a non-profit organisation registered in Africa to promote youth and rural empowerment, alleviate poverty in Africa through education, and improve the productivity and livelihood of farmers from subsistence to commercial farming in Africa.

He is a seasoned farmer and a prolific trainer. He is regularly interviewed on National Television for his outstanding service and achievement within the farming industry. He is also a regular writer and contributor to the International PigSite website.

He posted 150 videos on YouTube (papayemo1) covering the different aspects of pig farming. Over 2.5 million viewers watched the videos in over 36 countries, making it one of the most-watched pig farming videos on YouTube from an African perspective.

His Two Days Profitable Pig Farming training, which started over seven years ago, has trained more than 1,000 pig farmers in Nigeria, Togo, Cameroon and Ghana and has led to the establishment of 66 other farms across Nigeria and 3 in Ghana.

His book, "Profitable Pig Farming: A Step by Step Guide to Commercial Pig Farming from an African perspective" has become a must and a Blue Bible for those venturing into pig farming in Africa.

He is also the author of "Why Africa cannot feed itself and the way forward". The book considers all the factors causing the food crisis and food insufficiencies in Africa, such as geographical and environmental variables, climate change and historical factors like slavery and colonialism. Biological factors include food production rates and demographic and economic factors (such as population growth and urbanisation). Poor leadership and political failures, weak institutions. Poor implementation of market liberalisation reforms, prevailing external and macroeconomic factors, and different regions' socio-political situations. The book concludes with the way forward for Africa to become food sufficient and a bread basket for the world.

Mr Yemi, a diaspora, emigrated to the United Kingdom in 1991. He studied and worked for 20 years and earned his Master's in Business Administration and Master's degree in Social Work in the United Kingdom. In 2010, he emigrated to Nigeria to contribute to Nigeria's food production.

Acknowledgements

Although one man has written this book, it wouldn't have been possible without the many people who have been so inspirational and whose research and hard work was helpful during this book's writing.

I am thankful to God Almighty for His grace to research and put my findings into a book.

I also owe much to the many people who have encouraged me to follow my dream. In particular, my late dad, Mr. Solomon Olajide Adesina. And to Bola, my wife of 27 years of marriage, I thank her immensely for her undying love, support, and encouragement, which allowed me to travel, research, and practise farming in Africa for many years.

For my two sons, Femi and Seun, their input as second-generation African diaspora in the United Kingdom make the book more relevant to younger Africa. I want to thank them for the lengthy chat and healthy debate that we had late into the night and early morning to gather their perspectives on specific topics. I firmly believe their generation and beyond will move Africa further into the future.

Next, I would like to appreciate the hard work of my team at Pristine Integrated Farm Resources in Nigeria, Ghana, and Cameroon for organising farm training in their respective countries during my absence to allow me to focus on writing this book.

Many people influenced me to start looking at African challenges as a whole. Some of them I have met in person, and some I know through their teaching, lectures, training, research books and journals. They were from different walks of life. The variety of sources, expertise and professions assisted me in looking at the issue from several perspectives, which added lots of value to the book.

My initial inspirations were Pastor Matthew Ashimolowo, the late Dr Myles Munro, Dr Mensah Otabil, and Bishop Tudor Bismark. These pastors spent a lot of time teaching and believed that Africa could be better.

I am greatly indebted to Dr. Howard Nicholas, an economist and researcher at Erasmus University Rotterdam, The Netherlands, Lloyd Timberlake's book, "Africa in Crisis.". Jeffrey D. Sachs et al., for their input on the impact of geography. Jared Diamond's book on Guns, Germs, and Steel, Walter Rodney's book, "How Europe Underdeveloped Africa, Dr John Alembellah Azumah's book on the Legacy of Arab-Islam in Africa and Yemi Adeyemi, founder of ThinkAfrica.net, Sarah Barakat Obinna Anaekwe and Abdul B Parker for their input on Ancient African History

1. INTRODUCTION

"The nerve of the world has been deadened for centuries to the vibrations of African genius"

—*Late Ivan Van Sertima.*

As an African diaspora, I was fortunate to have spent almost half of my life in Africa and Europe. I could tell a lot about my adopted Continent's history, such as the rise and the fall of the Roman Empire, the British Industrial Revolution, the French Revolution, the Treaty of London, Henry VIII, the two World Wars and other European histories, but I know very little about the history of the African continent. In my discussion with my other African diaspora, I discovered that while most are learned and doing exploits in diverse fields of expertise, they know very little about African history. Some only know enough about the history of their African country and the region where their country is situated in Africa, but very little about other regions of Africa that are farther from their country of origin. This poor distribution of African knowledge was compounded by the fact that most African countries speak French or English as their primary national language, which means there is a limited knowledge transfer between countries, even among literate people within the Continent.

The greatest challenge is not the limited knowledge among first-generation immigrants but the scarcity of knowledge about Ancient African history that is passed on to the next generations of Africans. Those who know are often inundated with the day-to-day life and events of settling down in a foreign land and providing for their families that rarely have time to share African history with their children.

According to Dr Asa Hilliard- one of Africa's great educators, *"The education of African people is an urgent necessity. It is a matter of life or death, and we cannot afford the risk of another generation of children who have no identity and are ignorant about Africa."*

The late Professor Amos Wilson said, *"the purpose of education is not just to get a good job with great companies. The real purpose of education is to improve and further the interests of one's own group and to ensure its survival. The Indians, the Chinese, the Jews and other cultural groups have understood the importance of their history. They have worked extremely hard toward educating their children about their history from their perspective. African people have often looked at these cultural groups, marvelled at their unity, and wondered why it contrasts with their own community, which seems so fragmented and disorganized.*

The Holy Scripture also emphasises the need for a parent to always teach the next generation about their history. Genesis 18: 17 — 19 *And the LORD said, "Shall I hide from Abraham what I am about to do? 18Abraham will surely become a great and powerful nation, and ..... he will teach his children and his household after him ...."*

The need to share African history from an African perspective became more significant after watching a Science Channel documentary series hosted by Jack Turner in 2005 titled "What the Ancients Knew". The series visited key places from world history, focusing on the ancient civilisations' scientific, anthropological, economic, and mechanical issues and how their works influence modern life. Civilisations covered in the series include the Romans, the Greeks, the Egyptians, the Chinese, India, and the Japanese. The series overlooked the sophistication and impressive inventions of ancient Africa. But the reality is that most Greek and Roman discoveries came thousands of years after African developments.

This traditional Eurocentric perspective has dominated many history books taught in our schools and shown in our media, presenting Africans only as primitive victims of slavery without historical agency. Paul Gilroy describes this suppression of blackness achievement and contribution to the modern world as "cultural insiderism." Cultural insiderism is a condition in which people distinguish themselves from others with an absolute sense of difference to make themselves feel good at another group's expense, e.g. sense of ethnic difference.

This view of cultural insiderism was highlighted by an African novelist, poet, and critic, Chinua Achebe. He said that *"the last four or five hundred years of European contact with Africa has produced a body of literature that presented Africa in a very bad light and Africans in very lurid terms. The reason for this had to do with the need to justify the slave trade and slavery."*

The author of this book believes in the truism of the statement made by the late Ivan Van Sertima. *"The nerve of the world has been deadened for centuries to the vibrations of African genius"*.

This book aims to send an electrical impulse to this long-deadened nerve of African history. African history is significant, especially in understanding world history. Africa is home to the first humans. The Continent of Africa has the most extended human history because it has been around for a very long time. As a result, it is rich with the history of humanity and the origin of multitudes of civilisations. Some of the earliest archaeological discoveries of human development were found in Africa, including ancient cave paintings many thousands of years old.

France's Count Volney, scholar, Egyptologist and confidant of Benjamin Franklin, one of the Founding Fathers of the United States, once explained the conundrum of Africa in his book "Ruins of Empires.

"*In Egypt, I saw age-old monuments and temples lying half-buried in the sand and pondered the meaning of civilisation, its rise and its fall*". How is it that "*a people, now forgotten, discovered, while others were yet barbarians, the elements of the arts and the sciences? A race of men now rejected from society for their dark skin and frizzled hair, founded on the study of the laws of nature, those civil and religious systems which still govern the universe.*"

He continued, "*the Greeks had always given credit to the origin of their knowledge from Egypt's African and the hard evidence of the sphinx — whose features were clearly etched in the African mould — confirmed it. Was it not one of the crueller ironies of history that the people who had given the world civilisation were now race slaves and outcasts?*

In this book, our goal is to highlight some of the achievements of ancient black Africans and prove that the ancient people of Africa, like so many other ancients of the world, had great men and women who did great exploits and made a significant contribution to world civilisation. This book should go a long way to help young black people growing up around the world to feel confident and reassured that, contrary to popular opinion, they are descendants of people from ancient, rich and elaborate cultures that created a wealth of technologies in many areas. And for non-Africans, it will help eradicate misconceptions about black people and their history.

The book will also show that despite the suffering of black people through the horrific system of slavery and colonialism, Black Africans made and are still making countless contributions to science and technology, which we now enjoy today. Unfortunately, few African geniuses were recognised for their accomplishments, as the history of Africa is seldom publicised. Hopefully, this book will lead to more studies and discoveries in this area so that history can be put straight and more people will know more about the ancient African outstanding achievements.

In this book, the author presents the African story interestingly and factually to young people by looking at Africa's formation, geography, and impact on the planet on the ancient Africans. It also considers African societies' historical growth and development over thousands of years, focusing on the beginning of human history and how humans evolved from hunter-gathering to farming. And emphasise the ancient civilisation of Egypt, the first recorded monarch in human history and the development of African kingdoms and empires such as Mali, Songhai, Benin and Oyo Empire, and the continuing internal evolution of Africa's states. African belief cultures and their involvement in external trade.

The book also examines how traditional religions continue to coexist with Christianity and the influence of Islam on the cultural, political and economic and its dissemination and interaction with traditional African culture. Also, the impact of Europeans' trade network along West Africa and how this eventually led to the international enslavement of Africans. The long-term global consequence of enslavement laid the foundation of the present world economy with all its inbuilt inequalities. The European partition, conquest and occupation of Africa' from the 1880s, the impact of European commercial, religious and political presence during the Century, and Africa's changing role in the world economy as a producer of raw material and the consumer of European finished goods. The responses of African people to the challenges of colonialism, the growth of anti-colonial movements, and the state of Africa post independence.

Egypt was the first recorded monarch in human history. The ancient Africans built the city of Memphis in ancient Egypt in 3100 B.C. this was nearly 2000 years before any European civilisation. The Greeks built Athens in 1200 B.C., and the Romans built Rome in 1000 B.C.

Unlike the Greeks and Romans, the early African civilisation also had to invent things since they were the first and could not learn from other civilisations. Therefore, they were the first to discover the fundamental knowledge of medicine, mechanics and machinery (including ramps and levers), writing, paper, and all that goes for the continuation of a large organised society. Their exploration of the different fields of studies allowed them to create iconic inventions such as the pyramids, the first codified form of writing (hieroglyphics), the papyrus sheets, black ink, the calendar, and the clock name a few.

Chapter one looks at why it is important to teach African history that happened long ago from an African perspective. Chapter two sheds light on Africa's geography and some of the natural wonders that make the Continent unique. Chapter three looks at Africa as the origin of humans and the diversity of skin colour and languages that existed in Africa from the Founder effect on the continent.

Furthermore, chapter 4 examines how man evolved from hunter-gathering to domesticating plants and animals. Chapter five describes how the Ancient African civilization had to invent things for themselves from scratch because they were the pioneer of many discoveries. They were the first to discover metallurgy, astronomy, writing, paper, medicine, mechanics & machinery (including ramps, levers, ploughs and mills) and all that goes for the continuation of a large organized society. Their exploration of the different fields of studies allowed them to create iconic inventions such as the pyramids, the first codified form of writing (hieroglyphics), the papyrus sheets, black ink, the calendar, and the clock name a few.

Chapter 7 looks at how Ancient Africans domesticated and cultivated over 2,000 edible crops for over 3000 years. They include the finger millet, pearl millet, Emmer, Yams, Kolanut, Coffee and Sorghum. And how these domesticated crops could pave the road for future generations to live sufficiently depending on their agricultural products rather than spending billions on food.

Chapter 8 looks at the fact that humanity's origin is not restricted to East Africa alone but rather the entire continent of Africa. This section considers other areas of Africa where civilisation existed long before civilisation started in other parts, such as Egypt, Ethiopia, Nubia, Morocco, Western Sudan, and Zimbabwe, to give a snippet of Africa's economy and civilisation.

Chapter nine looks at many of the daily products created by African diasporas. Chapter ten tries to demystify one of the unfounded stereotypes that Africa's underdevelopment was caused by black proneness to drugs and alcohol abuse than other societies.

Chapter eleven looked at the two major slave trades in Africa. The trans-Saharan slave trade: slaves were taken from Africa to the Middle East and India by the Arabs from the 6th to the

15th century CE and also; the trans-Atlantic slave trade, or Euro-American slave trade, involved gathering, imprisoning, and transporting slaves from the African coast to the Americas. Chapter 12 looked at the impact that slavery had on Africa's population, farming, and economic development then and till the present.

Chapter thirteen looked at how colonialism tore Africa from its past, propelling the continent into a universe fashioned from outside that suppresses its values.

Chapter fourteen concluded the improvement in Africa, especially in Africa's ability to feed itself, and what the sub-Saharan Africa policymakers needed to do and put in place to build a modern, inclusive economy.

2. WHY TEACH AFRICAN HISTORY

"The only dark part of Africa is our lack of knowledge about it."

—*Dr. Jonathan Weaver*

Most people were falsely taught that the ancient Africans had little to do with the development and progression of civilisation. However, that's not right. Many recent scientific sources have proved that several advancements originated from Africa. Anthropological evidence proved that advances in various fields such as engineering, mathematics, navigation, writing, and arts occurred solely in African societies. Many essential things we utilise today should be credited to the ancient accomplishments of Africa's ancient civilisations.

The human species evolved on the Continent of Africa. The consequence is that Africa has been inhabited longer than any other place on Earth, so it's not surprising to learn that some of the greatest human inventors lived on this Continent.

The history of African inventors dates back to before modern humans technically existed. Our genetic ancestors, like Homo erectus, invented stone tools and discovered how to make fire. The fishing hook, bow and arrow, and even boats were first invented by Africans long before the advent of written history. Even as humans started migrating out of Africa, they took these ideas with them, and those remaining on the Continent continued inventing.

It is, therefore, essential to teach African history that happened long ago from an African perspective. History is inescapable; It studies the past and the legacies of the past in the present. History connects things through time and encourages learners to take a long view of such connections.

Winston Churchill stated, *"Those that fail to learn from history are doomed to repeat it."*

Machiavelli also reinforced this view: *"Whoever wishes to fore-see the future must consult the past; for human events ever resemble those of preceding times. This arises from the fact that they are produced by men who ever have been, and ever shall be, animated by the same passions, and thus they necessarily have the same results."*

Whether we like it or not, we are all products of living histories. The language we speak and the complex cultures, traditions and religions in our societies are products of the past. So also, the technology we use was formed in the past and perfected over time.

Research has shown that Africans are the most diverse people in the world — people with many skin tones. The diversity was because Africans were the earliest humans, and the Continent has witnessed several dispersions or migrations of people to other parts of Africa and the rest of the world. The scientist associated the diversity in Africa with a phenomenon called the " founder effect".

The founder effect is a phenomenon that occurs when a small group of individuals becomes isolated (or emigrated) from a larger population. Regardless of the original population, the new population will resemble only a few individuals that founded the smaller, distinct population. The diversity in Africa and humanity is due to the randomness that accompanies selecting and migrating a small group from a larger population to other parts of Africa and the rest of the Earth. The diversity further increases with the climatic effect and environmental changes, where the new colony found themselves and needed to adapt to the new and different environments. These factors account for the many skin tones of Africans, even within Africa, which ranges from very dark to very light, and the thousands of different cultures and languages spread across the Continent.

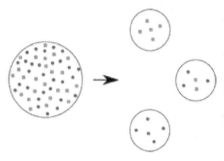
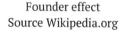

Founder effect
Source Wikipedia.org

Different African skin tones
Source thinkafrica.net

African history is significant, especially in understanding world history. Africa is home to the first humans. The Continent of Africa has the most extended human history because it has been around for a very long time. Africa has seen the rise and fall of many great civilisations and empires. The oldest and longest lasting of these are the Ancient Egyptians, still famous today for their pyramids and pharaohs. However, the Egyptians weren't the only civilisation developing in Ancient Africa. Important civilisations developed throughout the Continent, such as The Great Benin Empire, Great Zimbabwe empire, Empire of Mali, Empire of Songhai, and so many other great African civilisations, had a highly organised society that was developed, excelled in commerce and flourished

Unfortunately, Africa lost a huge part of her earliest history as they were passed orally from one generation to another due to the relatively short time for which writing has existed. Some parts of African history were also deliberately distorted and misrepresented. However, modern-day discoveries and methodology are helping to rediscover the lost pasts of Africa.

According to Dr Jonathan Weaver, *"The only dark part of Africa is our lack of knowledge about it."*

Africans have been interacting with the outside world for several millennia, and Africans exported essential minerals, agricultural products, labour skills and cultural expressions to the outside world. For example, it is a half-truth to talk about the Industrial Revolution in Europe without mentioning the 2 million Africans enslaved in America who produced cotton, which went into the 4,500 mills of Lancashire. And the enslaved people that worked in the sugarcane plantations produced sugar that improved the food taste in England. To miss such vital information when discussing industrialisation in Europe is not only wrong but a disservice to the next generation.

When young people are ignorant that Africans have always made good and valuable contributions to the world, they are automatically encouraged not to respect and appreciate Africans. The over-exposure through the news and popular media further reinforces this negative image of the disease, malnutrition, drought, political oppression, the lack of technological development, illiteracy and water pollution in Africa. The result is insensitivity, distrust and disdain towards black Africans worldwide.

While young people need to learn about these significant challenges and crises of Africa so they can respond effectively, there is a danger of creating an attitude of despair and hopelessness if this is the only aspect of Africa that is always portrayed to them in the media all the time. It is, therefore, essential to balance crises and challenges with good constructive and positive aspects such as Africa's growth and human development. Young people need to learn and appreciate the developments in African history and contemporary life throughout the Continent and how Africans have contributed positively to society, education, science, art, and medicine.

As in other continents, African people share commonalities that are desired by every human, e.g. the human drive for justice and freedom; the love of family and friends. The desire for good health care, education and adequate housing; the sadness of suffering from hunger, disease, natural disasters, or the loss of a loved one.

Providing young people with a balanced knowledge of Africa will allow them to see similarities and cultural differences between Africans and people of other races. It will also show that, just as siblings from the same parent look different and have different behaviour and character, they are still part of the same human family.

An ancient African proverb states, "it takes a whole village to raise a child." This is because our ancestors worked as a group and understood that it is important to invest the whole resource of the community in our children. In return, when the children reach adulthood, they would, in turn, do everything to promote not only their personal interests but the interests of the rest of the group. Our ancestors never left their children's education to chance because the future of their society's cohesiveness was of prime importance.

However, this is not the view many Africans and the African diaspora share these days. African communities have never had so many talented and educated economists, educators, sociologists, doctors, lawyers, artists, etc.. Yet, the continent still suffers the worst health, housing, and education. This is because education devoid of history might promote personal interests (with limited success) but will not promote our country or continent's interests.

Furthermore, more African people than ever in our history hold advanced degrees from some of the most prestigious Ivy League schools and universities. They can solve any myriad of problems for other groups, but since they have not received an African-centered education when it comes to their own, the result is limited.

Studies have shown that the more educated African people become, the more alienated they are from African culture. Sometimes in the bid to prove that they are better than their comrades, they promote interests that end up harming their people. That is why it is strange that despite African leaders' level of knowledge and education. Africa still allows agriculture and minerals to be exploited at Africa's expense (for our short-term and personal benefit).

In summary, young black learning about black African history creates a sense of belonging and makes them feel seen and for non-black, it will help eradicate any misconception they have about black people.

3. THE IMPACT OF AFRICA'S GEOGRAPHY ON AFRICAN DEVELOPMENT

"The study of geography is more than memorising places on a map. It's about understanding the complexity of our world and appreciating the diversity of cultures that exists across continents. And in the end, it's about using all that knowledge to help bridge divides and bring people together"

—*Barack Obama*

Geography studies the physical features of the Earth, its land, water and atmosphere, and its relationship with man's activities. Geography is the study of the relationship between the physical features of the Earth and humans. The word Geography originated from geo (Greek for Earth) + graphy (field of study) and was used for the first time around 2000 years ago by Eratosthenes, a Libyan mathematician in North Africa. It Geography includes weather conditions, climate and altitude. Many geographic factors affect agricultural businesses and trade. For example, specific climatic conditions in different geographical areas do determine or regulate which plant and animal can grow and flourish in a location. Therefore, agriculture is strictly bound to geography. Climate also impacts the key trade and shipping hubs (such as seas, oceans, lakes and rivers), shaping the development and fortunes of agricultural production of countries and continents.

In this chapter, we will look at Africa's geography and throw more light on all there is to know about some of the natural wonders unique to the Continent.

The geography of Africa is a significant factor that has positioned the Continent on a unique tangent regarding food production and economic development. To fully understand Agriculture in Africa, there is a need first to understand the physical Geography of Africa; and how this physical geography dictated and still dictates the growth and development of the Continent.

Africa is a unique and significant continent. It is the second-largest Continent in the world in size and population (after Asia), with an area of approximately 30.2 million km2 (11.7 million square miles), including adjacent islands. The size of Africa is 11.9 million square miles, which is around 11.5 billion football fields — each person of the 6 billion on Earth will get two football fields each from the size of land in Africa alone.

Africa's land size is larger than India, China, Mexico, the USA and a huge chunk of Europe combined. The Continent makes up nearly 15% of the world's population and covers 20% of the Earth's total land surface.

Geologists and historians believe that long ago, Africa was attached to all the other continents to form one gigantic continental landmass or supercontinent called Pangea, which made up one-third of the Earth's surface. Around 200 million years ago, the supercontinent broke into pieces through a weakness in the Earth's crust creating the volcanic rift zone. Over time, this rift zone would become the Atlantic Ocean.

The most visible evidence of this split is in the similar shape of the coastlines of modern-day Brazil and West Africa. The reconstructions showed that the contour similarity on the two continents was too good to be attributed to chance. That is, 200 million years ago, it would have been possible to walk or swim to Brazil from Nigeria during the Pangea period. The distribution of fossils across the continents also proves the existence of the supercontinent.

The breakup of Pangaea over time

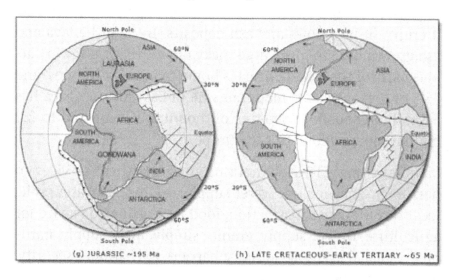

The breakup of Pangaea over time Source ornithology.com

As the Earth is divided up into different parts of the Earth's crust, the separate parts of each Earth's crust are called tectonic plates. These tectonic plates move in different directions due to convection in the Earth's inner layers. An earthquake is caused when these tectonic plates move against each other, stress builds up and is released in powerful waves of energy. However, where the tectonic plates run into each other, you get huge mountains, as in Europe.

Africa is the first Continent to be formed on Earth, so the tectonic table in the Continent is very stable. The ancient part of the Earth's continental crust that formed the land of the

African Continent did so a long time ago, between about 3.6 and 2 billion years ago. Unlike other continents, such as Asia and Europe, Africa rarely moves to cause earthquakes or volcanoes. All the continents' rocks have been extensively folded and metamorphosed by heat and pressure over time.

Volcanic mountain formation occurs when the Earth's magma works its way up to the surface, and once it gets to the surface, it erupts in lava flows and ash deposits. In time the lava and ash grow in size to form large rocky ranges that we see in various parts of the world. Africa is home to many volcanoes, and 75% of these volcanic mountains lie in East Africa. Africa has 3.0 million square kilometres of mountains compared to 2.2 million square kilometres in Europe.

Mountains provide a plethora of vital ecological services to humanity. They include water supply, driving the water cycle, locations for dam construction, food for grazing and space for agriculture, timber supply, granite supply, meat supply, natural ecological systems, military barriers for national security, biodiversity and recreational value.

Rivers also originate from mountains, and the tracks of water drainage create basins and watersheds that empty into the world's seas and oceans. These rivers are fundamental to agricultural activity. For instance, the Nile passing through Egypt and the largest lake in Ethiopia was from volcanic activity.

The Continent is bordered west by the Atlantic Ocean, previously called the Ethiopian Sea, in 1626. It is bordered north by the Mediterranean Sea and east by the Red Sea and the Indian Ocean (previously called the Azanian Sea). And on the south by the mingling waters of the Atlantic and Indian oceans.

Africa is divided almost equally in the middle by the Equator. Most of Africa lies within the Tropic of Cancer and the Tropic of Capricorn. Western Africa forms a bulge, meaning the greater part of Africa's territory lies North of the Equator. Africa is crossed from North to the south by the prime meridian (0° longitude), which passes a short distance to the east of Accra, Ghana.

Africa's major north-south axis is fundamental because as one travels along a north-south axis, one crosses zones that differ significantly in climate, habitat, rainfall, day length, and diseases of crops and livestock. Latitude is one of the major determinants of climate, growing conditions, and ease of spread of food production. Similar latitudes come with the same weather, and different longitudes come with varying weather conditions and patterns. Most of Africa's landmasses predominantly have a north-south axis, causing variation in what can grow in each country, from the Sahara in the North to the Savanna to the Forest in the South.

Furthermore, Africa's geography did shape the history and development of the culture and civilisations of the human race. Some African lands have been inhabited continuously by humans since the dawn of humanity. The geography impacted where people could live, important trade resources such as gold and salt, and trade routes that helped different civilisations interact and develop.

Ironically, when Africa is viewed on most maps, the Continent is presented as smaller than it is, and this is because the Earth is not a complete sphere. Also, most digital maps are made in two dimensions, so there will always be a risk of distortion while projecting valuable geographical information.

An excellent example of this discrepancy is the map designed by the European cartographer Geert de Kremer, better known as Mercator. Kremer drew the Mercator map for ship captains navigating the seas. The regions above or below the Equator appear more prominent than those located near the Equator. That is one of the main reasons why Africa seems smaller on Mercator-like maps, and the northern and southern extremities of the globe, such as, Canada, Russia, the United States, and Europe, were greatly enlarged and exaggerated. Africa, on the Equator, was significantly shrunk to fill the remaining gaps. As a result, the Mercator map portrays Europe's 3.8 million square miles to be larger than Africa's 11.9 million square miles.

In reality, three Canadas would comfortably fit inside Africa, and Greenland could fit into just one African country, the Democratic Republic of Congo. Unfortunately, the Mercator map has created an illusion in the mind of many young Africans that some European and North American countries are more prominent based on size. Ironically, even though we now have Satellite images of the Earth that show the accurate size of the Earth, the Mercator map remains a tool used to reinforce the supposed small size of Africa in the minds of Africans.

The map below shows the actual size of Africa compared to its false representation in the Mercator projection.

The climate of Africa is distinct and is influenced by several factors. First, Africa lies between 35° S and about 37° N latitude in the tropics. Second, the Equator divides the Continent into almost two halves. The third factor is the great east-west expansion of the continent North of the Equator, in contrast to its narrow width to the south. The narrow width means that the influence of the sea on the land is more felt in Southern Africa. Finally, the Continent's extensive plateau surfaces mean there are no high and long mountain ranges. As a result, climatic zones in Africa tend to phase into one another rather than change abruptly from place to place. The most critical differentiating climatic element in Africa is rainfall. The movement of air masses and their effects provide the basis for dividing the Continent into four distinct climatic regions.

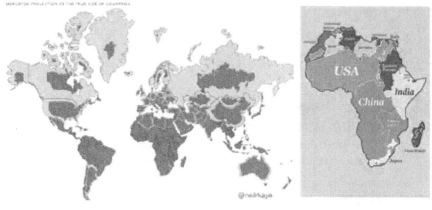

The True Size of Countries
Source thecoli.com

How big is Africa
Source Pinterest.co.uk

The Desert

The hot desert region consists of the Sahara and Kalahari deserts. The Sahara is the largest desert in Africa, and the largest hot desert in the world, with an area of 9,200,000 square kilometres, with summer temperatures reaching 50 °C — and stretching across 12 North African countries.

The Savannas

Savannah covers nearly half the total surface area of the African Continent as you move outward, outside the desert. African savannahs are classified as areas that receive between 300 and 1,500 mm of rain annually. African savannahs comprise 13.5 million km2. It is believed that Africa has around 600 million hectares of uncultivated arable land, approximately 60% of the global total. With such potential, Africa can become the food basket of the world. The savannas range from grassland plains with a few scattered trees, through scrub and open woodlands, to dense and complex systems of trees, bushes, and grasses.

African desert
Source afashionz.com

African Savannah
Souce wallpapercave.com

Equatorial Forest

The tropical Forest of Africa is mainly concentrated in a large block centred on the Equator, stretching inland as far as the mountains and highlands on the eastern boundary of the Zaire/Congo basin. This region is characterised by rainfall throughout the year but is heaviest in summer. The total area of the Forest is estimated to be about 1.6 million sq km, of which about one million sq km are in Zaire. Usually, the trees are tall and evergreen, rich in plant and animal life. As you move inward, away from the coast and north or south from the basin, the dry season becomes more pronounced, and the character of the forest changes and shades into the dry tropical forests and savannas of the interior.

Soil quality

Soil quality is the capacity of a soil to function within its ecosystem boundaries and interact positively with the environment external to that ecosystem. Incidentally, the African Continent's soil has been impacted far more by farming activity than any other continent. This is primarily because the span of human occupation in Africa exceeds that of any other continent. Farming activities like crop farming, grazing and browsing by livestock have severely depleted the quality of the soil and the natural vegetation, reducing tree cover and increasing grassland. Fifty-five per cent of the land in Africa is unsuitable for any kind of agriculture except nomadic grazing.

About 30% of the population, or about 250 million people, live in these poor-quality land resources. However, about 29% of the land has good quality soils, which cover 9 million km2 and support about 400 million people. The grounds enjoy adequate rain during the year, generally with a dry season of less than one or two months. At the same time, another 16 % or 4.7 million km2 of land has low-quality soils and currently supports about 200 million persons (23 %).

Most of Africa's soils are difficult to manage using the western system, and techniques developed by the west do not work well in Africa. The problem is not just in the ground but in the combination of soil and climate. Warm weather also breaks down organic matter quickly when water is present, so there is a quick but short-term release of nutrients as the rains begin in areas of short rainy seasons and long dry seasons. Heavy rainfall blasts away the lighter, more fertile humus, leaving heavier sand behind as the Sun dries it out. This problem is not easily cured simply by adding chemical fertilisers because there is little or no humus to hold the chemicals and keep them from being leached out of the root zone.

Most of the nutrients in a tropical forest system are contained in the living vegetation and the thick layer of decomposing matter on the forest floor. As soon as these trees are removed, and the soil humus is exposed, the thin layer of useful soil is quickly eroded by rainfall or depleted by farming.

Torrential rainfall
source Sauconsource.com

Gully Erosion
source bmrg.org.au

Finally, the rainfall pattern, especially the tropical rainstorms, tends to be extremely heavy, typically reaching 100 mm in half an hour. The rainfall is 80 times the amount in a typical London shower. The intensity of the rain causes the leaves to break and run down the trees' trunks, as long as the Forest is relatively intact. However, if the Forest is cleared and the trees are removed, the soil is carried away, and erosion becomes rapid and spectacular.

For these reasons, ancient African agriculture systems focused more on protecting the physical properties of the soil than its fertility. Our ancestors discovered that fertility was quickly used and could only be replaced by humus and soil nutrients replenishing. They realised that the most important thing is to ensure that the soil's physical property is not destroyed or made too sandy, laterite, or eroded to bedrock.

Shifting cultivation was developed and practised in Africa before colonisation to minimise the over-exposure of the land to environmental factors.

Another aspect of the Geography of Africa that affects its Agriculture negatively is that Africa happens to be the most landlocked Continent. Consequently, this impacted the spread and the movement of agricultural goods within the Continent. The size of the Continent and the lack of access to waterways made the movement of farming goods difficult within the Continent even today.

African rivers and lakes
source lizardpoint.com

African landlocks
source WorldAtlas

Being large and landlocked makes transporting and trading more expensive. It is usually more cost-effective and more accessible to transport goods over the ocean, sea, river, lake or canal than over land. Waterways give a significant advantage over hinterland economies. For example, the per-kilometre costs of overland trade within Africa are often three or four times greater than the costs of sea trade to an African port. The shipping of a six-metre-long container from Rotterdam in the Netherlands to Dar-es-Salaam in Tanzania — an air distance of 7,300 kilometres — was about $1,400. But transporting the same container overland from Dar-es-Salaam to Kigali, Rwanda — a distance of 1,280 kilometres less than a third by road — cost about $2,500, or nearly twice as much.

Lake and river

Where there is water, there is life. African rivers were significant in shaping the history of Africa in different areas. The Nile River was very important in the settlement patterns in Egypt. The Soil around the Nile River was very fertile and brought about settlements around that area compared to the more arid landscape in other parts of the country. The Nile river basin also served as the platform for the evolution and advancement of civilisation in the ancient world.

River Nile is the longest river in Africa and the world, with a length of 4,132 miles. Producing energy for the countries through which it flows. River Congo is the world's deepest and second longest river in Africa, with its depth reaching over 220m (720ft). River Niger is the eleventh longest river in the world. The third longest river in Africa is over 2,611mi (4,200Km).

Lake Victoria in East Africa stands as the largest lake in Africa and the largest freshwater lake in Africa, and it also is the second largest freshwater lake in the world.

There is also the uniqueness of Africa's river, which makes the transportation of Agricultural products even more daunting. For a river to be navigable, it must have a stable flow. Many African rivers have lots of water and flow too rapidly in floods during the rainy season, and most of them are dry or too shallow for navigation in the dry season. Most African rivers are also not navigable because many of these rivers, e.g. the Nile, the Niger and the Zambezi, have been dammed, diverted, and dredged to meet their water and energy needs.

There is also generally a high inland plateau in the South of the Equator. Some million years ago, the western part of Africa was moved up by tectonic forces, and the mouth of the big rivers suddenly found itself a few 100 metres above the sea. As a result, the rivers are forced to make a steep drop to a narrow coastal plain with huge waterfalls and rapids. Millions of years later, erosion has moved the river mouths more inland, but they can still not be sailed upon coming from the sea. There are too many meandering, too many waterfalls, sometimes too swampy, too narrow, too shallow, and they are too dry in dry seasons.

African waterfalls
Source depositphotos.com

Meandering river
Source dissolve.com

Prevalence of disease

Another unique way Africa's geography has hindered its development is in how its climate is suitable for the prevalence of certain diseases. Some infectious diseases are specific to the tropical and subtropical zones, such as malaria, which is transmitted by mosquitoes. The disease has never gained a lasting foothold in temperate zones. The cold winters naturally limit the activity of the mosquito insect that transmits the trypanosomiasis disease. Winter effectively controls the spread of the carrier, thereby limiting the spread of the disease in temperate countries. However, malaria is much more difficult to control in tropical regions because the weather suits the mosquito.

Before the discovery of Quinine as a malaria remedy, mosquitoes made Africa impenetrable to the Europeans, and Europeans only did business near the shore because of malaria and other diseases. Barely one in ten European explorers that ventured into Africa survived malaria and yellow fever. Thus, Europe nicknamed interior Africa "White Man's Grave."

It is exceptionally challenging to control malaria in tropical regions of Africa, where transmission occurs year-round and affects a large part of the population. According to the World Health Organisation, 300 million to 500 million new malaria cases occur annually. Almost all affected are knocked out for a week and are therefore incapacitated, most in bed or hospital. The recovery is followed by another two weeks when the patient is highly fatigued. The disease kills annually, as many as 2.3 million, and more than half of these are often young children. And for the young children who survive the malaria attack, it permanently stunts growth and lowers their Intelligent Quotient.

This widespread illness and early deaths have held back Africa's economic performance by significantly reducing farmers' productivity. But there are also long-term effects over time through various social feedbacks. For example, societies with high levels of child mortality tend to have high fertility levels: mothers bear many children to guarantee that at least some will survive to adulthood. Young children will therefore constitute a large proportion of that country's population. Low-income families cannot invest much in each child's education with so many children. High fertility also constrains the role of women in society because child-rearing takes up so much of their adult lives.

Other tropical diseases that are more common in the tropics include Yellow Fever, Chagas disease, African Trypanosomiasis (sleeping sickness), River Blindness, Schistosomiasis (snail fever), parasitic worms — roundworm, hookworm and whipworm. But most of the solutions to these problems are not insurmountable or expensive. For example, it is estimated that mosquito net halves Malaria infection in children and safe drinking water, sanitation and good toilet facilities could cut another infant mortality in half in much of Africa. Finally, handwashing can cut diarrhoeal diseases dramatically, by 40% in the under-5 age group.

Child washing hand
Source nestle.com

Child in mosquito net
Source trumpetnews.co.ug

The implication is not just the direct effect of the diseases, it also seriously affects economic development. For example, good health leads to productivity, and good productivity leads to wealth, leading to more taxes and an increase in a country's GDP. High GDP per capita feeds into good health through investment in medicine, public infrastructure, and just better health in general. That is a virtuous circle of how a good climate increases productivity and ultimately improves a country's GDP.

This page intentionally left blank

4. THE BASICS OF AFRICAN HISTORY

The name Africa is thought to be derived from different origins. One idea is that Africa comes from a Latin origin, from the word "aprica/apricus" meaning sunny. Another one is "afriki" formerly written "aphrike", of Greek origin. Aphrike is a name that is derived from phrike (cold). Phrike and the added negating prefix (a) give the meaning of 'without cold'.

As obvious as this might be, many people assume that Africa is a country. A good example is the Memorial Gates, mounted in the centre of London, where the names of the countries who contributed to the two world wars in defence of the British Empire. The countries were named as follows India, Pakistan, Sri Lanka, Bangladesh, Nepal and Africa. This juxtaposition of countries with a continent like this sometimes reinforces the misconception of Africa as a country in young people's minds. Africa is not a country but a diverse continent in language, geography, various urban and rural cultures, lifestyles and socioeconomic realities, religion, genetic variations and political ideas.

The continent is made up of 56 nations, the most in any continent, followed by Asia with 47 countries and Europe with 43 countries. The table below shows the total breakdown of the number of countries in each Continent.

Continent	Number of Countries
Africa	54 countries
Asia	47 countries
Europe	43 countries
North America	23 countries
Australia and Oceania	14 countries
South America	12 countries
Antarctica	0 countries

Population — Asia has 62% of the world's population, with over 4 billion people. Africa follows this with over 1 billion people, amounting to about 16% of the world's population. Europe comes third in population size with about 700 million people and 8% of the world's total population. Others are North America with 500 million, South America with 400 million, Australia and Oceania with 36 million, and Antarctica with 4 thousand.

Country size — **The Largest country in Africa by population is** Nigeria, with 200,003,000 people. Ethiopia follows this with a population size of 103,764,000, and then Egypt.

The Largest country in Africa by GDP is Nigeria, with a total estimated Nominal GDP of $376.284 billion in 2017. South Africa followed with a GDP of $349.299 billion. Other countries are Egypt, Algeria, Angola, Morocco, and Ethiopia.

The Largest country in Africa by area is Algeria, the 10th largest in the world, with 2,381,741 square kilometres. The Democratic Republic of the Congo has 2,344,858 square kilometres, and Sudan with 1,861,484 square kilometres.

Languages — Africa is home to over one-third of the world's total languages (about 6,000 languages worldwide). Despite the bilingual nature of Europe, which can be attributed to Europe's closeness of countries, it only accounts for about 300 languages worldwide. Africa is multilingual, with some areas like western Uganda having each person speaking an average of 4 languages.

Why does Africa have so many languages?

The Christian explanation is found in the book of Genesis, Chapter 11: 1- 9. The Bible stated that there was a period when the entire world spoke one language. This unity among all humans led to a case of self-idolatry, unwillingness to obey God's command to populate the Earth, and an ambition to take pride in their achievements rather than reverencing God. God decided to humble humans by confounding their language, which led to the scattering of humans abroad upon the face of the whole and gave rise to the different groups and languages developed on Earth.

The scientists attribute Africa with creating not only the first language but also the first language group developed by *Homo sapiens 340,000 years ago, amounting to more than 17,000 generations.* With over 2,000 living languages, language diversity in Africa supports the genetic evidence that positions Africa as the cradle of the human species based on the founder effect. The African Continent has experienced a lot of migrations; Africans from Morocco moved Northeast and West of Africa. Those from the Eastern part moved into West Africa, and even Africans from West Africa, East Africa, and North Africa migrated through the Arabian Peninsula into Europe, Asia, Oceania, and even the Americas. This migration and mingling of cultures contributed immensely to the linguistic diversity in Africa.

Religion — Africa is home to many religions and beliefs and houses a mixture of local and global beliefs. One cannot generalise the nature of African religions as this would lead to the mistake of homogeneity among all African cultures. Although religion in Africa is multifaceted, it has primarily influenced the Continent's art, philosophy, and culture. In today's Africa, various individuals adhere to mainly Christianity, Islam, and to some lesser extent, traditional African beliefs. Some religions are unique in Africa.

At the core of many traditional African beliefs is a belief in an all-powerful distant Creator. This Creator supersedes all spirits responsible for controlling 'principles'. The Creator also supersedes ancestors and gods, responsible for cross-generational blessings or curses. The ancestors, spirits and king are the mediators between the people and the most powerful.

For example, the Creator among the Yorubas is Eledumare (Creator of everything in the world) and Olorun (ruler of the heavens). Spirits called Orishas can also travel between the heavens and the Earth. Examples include Sango, Orunmila, Osanyin, Esu, Erinle, Osun, Ogun, Oya, and many others.

Generally, religion is vital to Africans. A survey conducted by the Pew Research centre shows that most African (about 95%) believe in one form, the main religions being Christianity and Islam. On the frequency of prayer, most Muslims affirmed that they pray five times daily. The Christians, for instance, pray anytime in the day; Sunni Muslims pray five times, while Shia Muslims pray three times a day.

Africans hold fasting very high, especially for the Christians, during lent and general fasts by churches and the Muslims during their Ramadan fast.

Most traditional worshippers (even Christians and Muslims), tend to hold high certain concepts and beliefs. For example, many believe in using Juju, shrines and other sacred objects to protect them from harm.

The uniqueness of Africa to human history

Two unquestionable fact that all scientists do agree on is that all modern humans emanated from Africa and that there is more genetic variation amongst humans in Africa than amongst the non-African population due to the founder effect. According to scientists, humans lived side by side for longer in Africa than outside Africa, amounting to 1.5 million years within Africa, compared to shorter periods for human remains found outside Africa.

Our earliest ancestors had an overabundance of behaviours that made them more successful in populating the Earth in significant numbers. Archaeologists believe the fire was first lit in East Africa around two million years ago, and this discovery remains one of the most ground-breaking events in the development of humanity. Fire gave humans an advantage over all other animals: they could cook with it, which aided in the quick digestion and absorption of most of their meat, making digestion faster. Unlike other predators, which had to sleep for hours to digest their food, man could stay awake longer. Staying awake longer meant humans could think longer, be more creative, and keep warm in all environments. They also discovered fishing and developed language, art, paint-making, religion, abstract thinking, timekeeping (Ishango bone), and mathematics (Lebombo bone). Caring for the sick and infirm, sculptures of figurines, developed collective learning, hunting animals, gathering edible plants and making ornaments.

There are suggestions that after the human ancestors shed most of their body hairs, they quickly evolved dark skin for protection against U.V. radiation from the Sun. All humans were originally black; white skin only appeared in higher frequencies around 8,000 years ago. DNA evidence shows that skeletons from earlier than 8,000 years in Spain, Hungary, and Luxembourg (Central and Southern Europe) were brown-skinned. An example is the Cheddar man, the oldest skeleton of the human species in the United Kingdom was found in Somerset, in the heart of England. His genetic markers indicated that he was dark-skinned, with dark brown hair and blue eyes. The Cheddar man is an early indication that Africans or descendants did live in Europe and were a part of its population. Cheddar man is believed to have lived 10,000 years ago. This discovery is consistent with some other Mesolithic human remains discovered throughout Europe. The genetic information for lighter skin was already present amongst the Africans before humans emigrated to Asia, Europe and America, later manifested on human skin as they moved farther away from the hot Equator.

Cheddar man from Sommerset
Source — haplogroup.blogspot.com

An illustrative statute of Cheddar man from Sommerset, England, 10,000 years ago

Who is an African?

The answer to this question looks straightforward, but the reality is that the answer becomes less evident once you start looking closely at answering the question.

Professor Ali Mazrui classified Africans into Africans of the blood and Africans of the soil". Africans of the blood are defined in racial and genealogical terms. These are those born to an African parent, either first, second or third generation or those with an African passport, usually dark skin. Those born in Africa hold the citizenship of African countries or have ancestry in the Continent as African. At the same time, Africans of the soil are those who live in Africa in geographical terms.

Many erroneously assume that Africa is a continent of dark-skinned people. For example, assuming a white UK police officer radioed the scene of a crime, thus: "At the scene of the crime were four Africans and four white boys." What thoughts and images come to your mind to differentiate the four 'Africans' from the four White boys?

Generally, the first thought that comes to most people's minds is a mental image of a dark-skinned person. But the reality is that there is no such race as the African race. There are many natural African skin tones ranging from very dark to very light, skin as light as some Asians to the darkest skin on a global level and everything in between. The African Continent contains thousands of social groups entirely different in culture, language, and even physical appearance.

Skin colour results from diversity due to mutations. The emergence of 4 depigmentation genes began between 8,000 to 11,000 years ago. These pigments help the human body use the Sun's vitamin D even at low UV exposure latitudes.

As mentioned earlier, after the human ancestors shed most of their body hair, they quickly evolved dark skin for protection against U.V. radiation from the Sun. Subsequent migrations from the Equator towards the North and south poles led early humans to gradually transit to a lighter skin tone. Africans with the lowest melanin levels were found to be mainly in Southern Africa, while individuals with the highest melanin concentration were in Eastern Africa. Within these two regions consist of a variety of different shades of skin tones. The skin colour is highly variable on the African Continent and is still evolving."

Three main factors naturally determine skin colour in humans, including genetics, level of exposure to Sun and concentration of melanin on the skin.

Genetics

The gene mutations that determine the lighter skin tone of Europeans are of African origin, called SLC24A5. The gene has swept and evolved across Europe for the past 6000 years. This pigment is commonly present in Africans, especially in East Africa and Ethiopia. More than half of the members of some Ethiopian groups carry this SLC24A5 gene, although they do not have white skin.

Exposure to the Sun

There is also a direct correlation between the geographical reception of ultraviolet radiation from the Sun and indigenous skin pigmentation. People closer to the cold North and south poles tend to tilt towards lighter skin tones, while people closer to the hot Equator tend to have darker tones.

Melanin

Finally, melanin is also a significant factor in determining skin colour; it is a pigment produced by the body within the skin that determines skin colour, eye colour, and hair colour—albinism results from the absence or very little presence of this pigment in an individual.

Researchers and scientists have reported that humans from all over the planet over millenniums, as they migrated and settled to areas with different intensities of U.V. radiation, have transitioned from dark-skinned to light-skinned and vice versa. The transitioning process usually takes about 100 generations or approximately 2,500 years for a complete skin tone change.

Many past European-based historians usually characterise a black African as someone who possesses thick lips, a broad nose, jet black skin, and woolly hair. However, this description only fits Africans from the West and Central African lineage, which is less than half of Africa.

When North, South and East Africans are added to who is an African, then a black African is also someone with light skin, a thin nose, and straight hair.

There are lots of black Africans in North Africa, and for a long time, this has been a mixture of black Africans, lighter skin Africans and mixed Africans. The proportion of black Africans in North Africa (Morocco, Algeria, Libya, Tunisia and Egypt) fell between 5,000 BCE and 650 AD, due to fleeing invasions (as refugees or internally displaced persons) from the Hyksos, Persians, Greeks, Romans, Byzantines, and Arabs during the Islamic conquest.

Who were the Egyptians that built Ancient Egyptian civilisation?

Undoubtedly, some Ancient Egyptians from 5,000 BCE to 305 BCE were black though some were not. Many historians struggle to associate Egypt's great civilisation with the black people. This section looks closely at the skin pigmentation of the ancient Egyptian civilisation.

As we mentioned, Black just means a person with a brown complexion. This could be a light complexion like the San people or a dark complexion like the Mulatto to Jet Black. or woolly hair. Modern Egyptians and some North Africans have a lighter black complexion.

The four genes associated with depigmentation are KITLG, TYRP1, SLC24A5, and SLC45A2. The three genes responsible for lighter skin complexion were first developed at latitudes far from the Equator around 11,000 years ago to 19,000 years ago — KITLG, TYRP1, SLC24A5, and SLC45A2. These genes started spreading to most Europeans and Asians 8,000 years ago, and De-pigmentation spread to the black Egyptians from the Near East through interbreeding.

We saw evidence of this in the Bible. For example, as a way of binding peace treaties, the Pharaohs and daughters of Pharaohs often married royalty from neighbouring countries, resulting in "mixed race" children. A famous example is one of the wives of King Solomon in the bible, who was a daughter of the Pharoah of Egypt (1 Kings 3:1), about whom Songs of Solomon was written.

Song of Solomon 1: 5 "I am black but comely, O ye daughters of Jerusalem, as the tents of Kedar, as the curtains of Solomon. 6 Look not upon me; I am black because the sun hath looked upon me.....

The spread of these genes maximised vitamin D synthesis for humans far away from the Equator.

ANCIENT TESTIMONIES ABOUT THE ANCIENT EGYPTIANS THE FROM OTHER CULTURES

There are many references in writing by other cultures which describe the real Egyptians in terms of their complexion. Here are some of the best documented and earliest in the world:

1. **Pliny the Elder, Natural History, Book 2, 77 A.D.** "For it is beyond question that the Ethiopians [i.e. Africans] are burnt by the heat of the heavenly body near them, and are born with a scorched appearance, curly beard and hair..."

2. **Herodotus, The Histories, Book 2, 450 BCE** "There can be no doubt that the Colchians are an Egyptian race. Before I heard any mention of the fact from others, I had remarked it myself... My own conjectures were founded on the fact that they are black-skinned and have woolly hair..."

3. **Galen, Mixtures, Book 2, 1st Century A.D.** "The hair of Egyptians... and in general all peoples who inhabit hot, dry, places, has poor growth and is black, dry, curly, and brittle."

4. **Diodorus Siculus, General History, Book 3, 30 BCE** "Now the Ethiopians, as historians relate, were the first of all men and the proofs of this statement, they say, are manifest... They also say that the Ethiopians are colonists sent out, Osiris having been the leader of the colony."

5. **Herodotus, Book II p.100 translated b George Rawlinson, New York: Tudor, 1928** "The Egyptians have burnt skin, flat noses, thick lips, and woolly hair" Readers may wish to obtain the book "Return To Glory". The book, written by a white author and professional speaker Joel F. Freeman, discusses the

historical and archaeological evidence for ancient black Egyptian civilisation.

6. Physiognomics, anonymous writing attributed to Aristotle, late 3rd century/ early 2nd century "Those who are too dark are cowardly; witness Egyptians, Ethiopians."

Testimony of Egyptologists

France's Count Volney, scholar, world traveller, a confidant of Benjamin Franklin and an aristocrat of pronounced republican sympathies, once explained the conundrum. *"In Egypt, he had seen age-old monuments and temples lying half-buried in the sand and had pondered the meaning of civilisation, its rise and its fall. How is it, that "a people, now forgotten, discovered, while others were yet barbarians, the elements of the arts and the sciences. A race of men now rejected from society for their dark skin and frizzled hair, founded on the study of the laws of nature, those civil and religious systems which still govern the universe. Was it not one of the crueller ironies of history that the people who had given the world civilisation were now a race of slaves and outcasts?*

Skull examinations

During the early 20th Century, paleoanatomists examined many ancient Egyptian skeletons and attempted to categorise the Egyptian skull samples using their craniometric criteria for racial classification. Faulkenburger, using his own parameters, classified pre-dynastic skulls as 36 per cent Negroid, 33 per cent Mediterranean, 11 percent Cro-Magnoids and 20

Sculptures and reliefs

The Egyptians provided evidence that they were aware of skin colour, symbolism, facial features, hair, costumes, context and materials (tools, weapons, gifts and other items). One of the sources of division is the claim that Egyptians painted themselves red. The following pictures demonstrate that what some academics describe as red, "Mediterranean" or dark red instead of brown, is ethically dishonest.

Dark brown skin colour used to depict the ancient Egyptians.

Bust of Tutankhamun
Source Cairo Museum

Dark brown and medium brown skin tones of Ancient Egyptians were found in the royal tombs, and the dark brown skin colour was used to depict the ancient Egyptians. Cairo Museum.

Bust of Tutankhamun and Queen Ahmose Nefertari and King Amenhotep, her son. Mentuhotep II, the sixth ruler of the 11th dynasty, ruled from around 2061 to 2010 BCE and is credited with reuniting Ancient Egypt and Pharaoh Amenemhat III (1859-1813 BC)

Queen Ahmose Nefertari and King
Amenhotep

Mentuhotep II
Source ThinkAfrica

DNA Analysis of Ancient Egyptians

The result of the first DNA tests done on royal mummies in 2010 settled the dispute concerning the ethnicity of the ancient Egyptians by scholars in the 20th Century. This dispute was solved scientifically by the DNA tests conducted on the mummies of Pharaoh Rameses III and his son in 2012 and 2013. The DNA tests proved they belonged to the human Y chromosome group E1b1a and 50% of their genetic material. This is the Y chromosome group of Sub-Saharan Africans who speak Niger-Congo. This meant that Ramses III and his son carried the same haplogroup as Nelson Mandela. Sub — Saharan DNA — Haplogroup E originated in the Horn of Africa which is in "Sub-Saharan Africa ", and is now found all over North Africa and different parts of the world.

5. HOW AGRICULTURE BEGAN IN AFRICA

"There is no question that Africans contributed towards the development of human beings as we know them today. They were the first to use their physical capabilities to enlarge their brains. They were able to develop the technology of stone tools. They were the first ones to move out of trees and walk upright. And they were the first ones to explore?. Crossing the seas and going out to Asia and Europe... and to me this is the greatest achievement that humanity has ever done."

—George Abungu,
of the National Museums of Kenya

It is a scientific fact that humans first evolved in Africa, and much of human evolution occurred on the Continent. However, the Geography of Africa, especially its impact on man's early farming activities, forced humans to move from one place to another and, finally, out of the Continent to other parts of the Earth. Understanding early man's relationship with his environment is needed to understand the history of Agriculture in Africa.

As mentioned earlier, African ancestors were the first humans to use their physical capabilities to enlarge their brains. Archaeologists believe the first fire was lit in East Africa around two million years ago. Interestingly, the discovery of fire helped man develop faster than any other factor. It allowed humans to cook, which aided in the quick digestion of most of their meat and staying awake to be more creative and keep warm in all environments.

How weapons evolved   Neolithic farm settlement
Source timetoast.com   source liboom.com

Over time, humans developed their hunting and foraging skills. They invented the use of projectiles. Projectiles are weapons that can be thrown with which they could use to attack animals from a distance. This basic technology made it easy for the community to plan and better organise themselves for hunting and foraging. It reduced the risks of unpredictable environmental changes and encouraged migration around the planet.

Initially, our ancestors tended to seek out and hunt only smaller animals, such as rodents and use clubs to kill them. They would avoid attacking larger animals such as giraffes, zebras, or elephants not to get injured; instead, they wait for them to be killed by other beasts or die of natural causes.

However, between 50 thousand years ago, humans developed more sophisticated tools, shaping stone points as spearheads and creating bows and arrows. The spears are usually tipped with vegetable poison to aid the speed of the animal's death. They also used a wide range of implements made of bone used as needles or fish hooks.

Based on evidence found at one of Africa's most important geological sites, Olduvai Gorge in Tanzania, these humans constructed small structures of tree branches as shelter. The size of the shelters would suggest they lived in small family groups and that each family would have its residential unit.

Pygmy hunter-gatherers
source bing.com

Pygmy hunter-sun-dried meat
source bing.com

Humans have always moved from one place to another, hunting and gathering food. One of the reasons for migration is environmental stress and population increases. When resources, primarily food and water, become insufficient, people move to find and inhabit areas that are good for farming and livestock raising.

A group of 150 to 1,000 people is said to have crossed through the Middle East from northeast Africa before spreading throughout Eurasia around 60,000 years ago.

Climate change is another reason why humans left Africa. Man thrives and flourishes in a climate with lots of rainfall, as rainfall largely determines the kind of plants that will grow in a particular place, ultimately determining the food our ancestors would eat for sustenance. Any significant changes to the rainfall pattern affect this system adversely, therefore forcing our ancestors to move

Unfortunately, in the past, the weather system changed all the time. For instance, Earth lapsed into a wobble 20,000 years ago while spinning around the Sun. As a result, its orbit strayed farther out into space than usual. The wobble led the planet into an ice age that changed the entire world's rainfall, weather patterns, ecosystems, and biodiversity, making things too cold and unfavourable for humans. Climate change is not new to the Earth, as ice ages tend to occur regularly in the past and last for tens of thousands of years.

Archaeologists believe that the ice age affected the climate of northeast Africa and led to the emigration of humans across the Sahara desert. The Sahara in the northeast of Africa (the main path through to the Middle East) is prone to the formation of desert, which was impenetrable to our ancestors — specifically the Saharan and Arabian desert. However, following the ice age period, parts of northeast Africa became lush with vegetation. The area flourished with rich ecosystems, forming a route — green corridors — between Africa and the Middle East and making a penetrable route favourable for human migration. Scientists have found many seashells in the heart of the Sahara Desert, and there is no way they could be there except if large bodies of water have passed through the desert.

Paleogeographic map showing
possible ostracode migration routes
Source Researchgate

Trans-Sahar Seaway 56-66m years ago
source novataxa.blogspot.com

Paleogeographic map showing possible ostracode migration routes from central West African basins to northeast African basins (after Morsi and Speijer, 2003) and the trans-Sahar Seaway 56 -66m years ago Some of the sea creatures that lived underwater in the location where the Sahara desert is today. Photograph: American Museum of Natural History 2019.

As mentioned earlier, climate change has been a great set of traffic lights for human migration. There was a red light for immigration when deserts stretched thousands of miles across northern Africa. It was a green light for migration when a wet climate flourished with plants, and lush ecosystems started growing in the Sahara desert.

Most evidence of agriculture before the 4th millennium BCE in the Sahara Desert is likely to be buried beneath the desert. Though around 6,000 years ago, Lake Chad used to be an inland sea called Lake Mega-Chad by scientists. The lake supported societies that left a material culture today called the Sudanic Aquatic Tradition, innovators in fishing and pottery dating back to 6,000 BCE.

The shrinking of Lake Mega-Chad, desiccation of the Sahara, and climate change had consequences for ancient African ancestors and they had to relocate.

This page intentionally left blank

6. WHAT THE ANCIENT AFRICAN KNEW ABOUT MANUFACTURING.

European and North American scholars have defined civilisation in the last few centuries. As such, it is weighted towards cultural achievements that indicate the early achievement of civilisation. As a result, Africa's contributions to human advancement are often downplayed. European would readily acknowledge the contribution of ancient Greece as the foundation upon which they built their development, but that credit is never extended to Africa.

In ancient Africa, "manufactures" literally meant "things made by hand," and African manufacturers, in this sense, have advanced appreciably.

Most African societies met their own needs for various household items, farming tools, and weapons. One way of judging Africa's level of economic development five centuries ago is by the quality of the products. For example, in North Africa, Europeans became familiar with a superior brand of African red leather called "Moroccan leather." It was tanned and dyed by Hausa specialists in northern Nigeria and Mali. And again, when the Portuguese first reached the old kingdom of Kongo, they sent back word of the superb local cloths made from bark and palm fibre, having a finish comparable to velvet. Africa was manufacturing superior cotton cloth from the Guinea coast, which was said to be stronger than Manchester cotton.

Before writing was invented, Africans had made some advancements that we now take for granted today. They include fire, clothing, art, painting, hunting animals, gathering edible plants, mathematics, fishing,. Humans that left Africa took these ideas to the rest of the world.

CALENDAR

The Ancient Egyptian Star Chart
Source ThinkAfrica

Modern calendar
Source designhunter.co.uk

If you were asked to guess who invented the 365-day calendar, you would probably answer without hesitation that it was the Roman, and you would be wrong. The Romans only started to have a world influence during the 3rd Century, and they started off using a lunar calendar based on ten months and 304 days introduced by Romulus, the founder of Rome.

However, Ancient Africa had already invented a 365-day calendar before this period.

The number of hours in a day is determined by the time it takes a planet to spin around its axis. For example, on Venus, a day is 5,832 hours; on Mercury is 1,408 hours; on Mars is 25 hours; and on planet Earth, it is 24 hours.

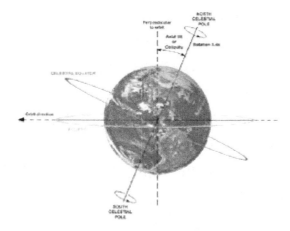

Africa, the origin of the 365-day calendar
source Thinkafrica

The calendar we all use today is the solar calendar, and it was invented in Egypt. The calendar had religious, political and agricultural significance in Egypt. The year usually starts in July when the Nile deposits silt and water to facilitate irrigation and productive plant cultivation by the Egyptians. Egypt then picked a solar calendar, in which one year represented one orbit around the Sun by the Earth.

In the beginning, the solar calendar has 12 months and 30 days each throughout the pharaonic period. Later, the solar calendar system was revised and became the basis of today's Western calendar.

The word calendar comes from Latin, meaning "call", announcing the start of a new year.

- Januarius, written mensis Januaris, Janus was the god of beginnings

- Februarius comes from Februum, a month of ritual purification.

- March came from the Latin Martius mensis, meaning the month of the god Mars.

- April came from Aprilis in Latin — the month of Venus (Aphrilis in Latin).

- June came from mensis Junius, which contained the summer solstice

- July was named after Julius Caesar, after deification for conquering France.

- August was named after Augustus for being one of the best Roman emperors.

- September is from Latin for the seventh (Septem) month (-ber).

- October is from Latin for the eighth (Octo) month (-ber).

- November is Latin for ninth (Novem) month (-ber)

- December from Latin for the tenth month.

ASTRONOMY

Around 2000 years ago, Eratosthenes, born in 276 BC in Libya in North Africa, calculated the spherical size of the Earth. He calculated it with considerable accuracy by comparing the position of the Sun's rays in two locations.

Eratosthenes created a mathematical method still used today, known as the "Sieve of Eratosthenes". The method involves an algorithmic system that he designed for finding prime numbers, which are whole numbers that are only divisible either by themselves or by the number one. Eratosthenes invented a system of latitude and longitude, and he was the first to calculate the tilt of the Earth's axis with remarkable accuracy. He also calculated the distance between the Earth and the Moon and the distance between the Earth and the Sun. Eratosthenes solved the equation to find that the Earth's circumference is 250,000 stadia or 40,000 Km.

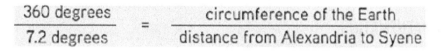

$$\frac{360 \text{ degrees}}{7.2 \text{ degrees}} = \frac{\text{circumference of the Earth}}{\text{distance from Alexandria to Syene}}$$

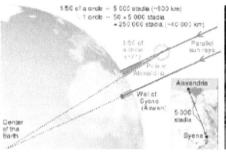

Eratosthenes Measure
The Circumference of Earth
Source ThinkAfrica

Hobble Telescope
Source worldatlas.com

ABSTRACT ART

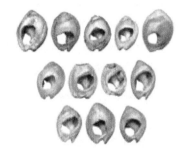

Cave of Pigeons Taforalt, Morocco

Ancient Shells Discovered in Morocco
Source atlasobscura.com

Contrary to the common belief that abstract art did not start in European countries, archaeological evidence revealed that Africa was the home to abstract art nearly 73,000 years ago in the Blombos cave of South Africa, and ornamental shells were discovered in Morocco. Many of these are displayed in European museums. Artists like Pablo Picasso first recognised and admired African art for its unique beauty, spirituality and various uses.

MATHEMATICS

Geometry Ancient Egypt
Source rogerburrowsimages.com

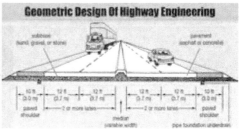

Highway engineering
Source Engineeringdiscoveries.com

According to Paul Gerdes, the concept of geometry started early in African history. Africa is where humans learned to use geometric thinking in their day-to-day life. For example, the hunter-gatherers of the Kalahari Desert often learned the shape to track animals and to determine the kind of animal that passed by, how long ago, etc. Ancient Rock paintings and engravings from all over Africa indicated geometrical explorations by African hunters, farmers and artisans.

The Ishango bone is a prehistoric artefact, and the oldest table of prime numbers discovered in northeastern Congo is estimated to be 20,000 years old or more. Eight thousand years ago, people in present-day Zaire developed their own numeration system, as did Yoruba people in what is now Nigeria. The Yoruba system was based on units of 20 (instead of 10) and required an impressive amount of subtraction to identify different numbers. For example, the base of the counting system in Yoruba is *ogún* 'twenty' (or 'score'). To count from 1 to 10, units in 1–4 are created by adding to these, while units in 5–9 are created by subtracting from the next decade. The odd decades are created by subtracting ten from the next even decade. Multiples are also very important in the numerical system. For example, the number 60 is ọgọ́ta which means three twenties (ogún = 20, ẹ̀ta = 3). In other words, your addition and subtraction must be good to do basic counting in the Yoruba language.

The most ancient mathematical documents available are Egyptian papyri from 2000 – 1800 BC, the Rhind Mathematical Papyrus and the Moscow Mathematical Papyrus. They contained complex problems in arithmetic, algebra and geometry, the different methods for solving them, and detailed explanatory theories. Ancient Africa understood basic algebra and geometry concepts and could solve simple sets of simultaneous equations. They were able to estimate the area of a circle by subtracting one-ninth from its diameter and squaring the result:

$$\text{Area} \approx [(^8/_9)D]^2 = (^{256}/_{81})r^2 \approx 3.16r^2,$$

A reasonable approximation of the formula πr^2.

The mathematical ability was evident in many Egyptian constructions, including the pyramids.

ALGORITHMS

You are probably working or reading this book from kindle in your home or office, your smartphone or computer links with satellites in orbit, and artificial intelligence performs a wide range of tasks towards achieving your goals. But you could not achieve all these feats without a fundamental mathematical principle, underlying instructions, and an algorithm. An algorithm basically means an established, detailed, structured step-by-step instruction to solve a problem or carry out a task. This idea originated and was invented by Africans.

Kindle and smartphone

This is not to say that Africans originated step-by-step instructions for the complex computer. We are referring to the earliest established mathematical principles by which most machines operate, mathematical algorithms. The set of mathematical rules which form the bases of most inventions was started in Africa by Africans thousands of years ago.

The Rhind Mathematical Papyrus   Moscow Mathematical Papyrus
Source ThinkAfrica

According to history, the Greeks learnt, built and expatiated on what they learnt in Egypt but always recognised the education they acquired from ancient Egypt. The civilisation built the Sphinx, raised the pyramids, and founded geometry and astronomy. Greek scholars like Thales, Plato, Pythagoras, Hippocrates, and Socrates travelled to Egypt to study and learn. It was in Egypt that Pythagoras learned calculus and geometry. "Egypt was the cradle of mathematics," wrote Aristotle.

This mathematical Papyrus proved that Africans created the algorithm, which over the years, became the bases of most inventions.

PAPER

Papyrus plant   Printing press
Source bing.com   source hamarlaser.com

Until recently, newspapers and textbooks have been responsible for shaping our educational and public opinion, which is the cornerstone of democracy. The ancient Egyptians published papyrus and water hyacinth leaves for thousands of years.

Papyrus, from which the English word "paper" is derived, is the writing material of ancient times. Papyrus was manufactured in Egypt as far back as the fourth millennium BCE. It was made from the papyrus plant's pith, the aquatic plant Cyperus papyrus, also known as the paper plant. The plant was indigenous to the Nile delta region in Egypt and was collected mainly for its stalks. The central pith of those stalks was cut, pressed and finally dried to form a thin, smooth writing surface.

The papyrus paper was the main writing material in ancient Egypt, and later it was adopted by the Greeks and the Roman Empire. It was used for correspondence, legal documents and for producing books like rolled-up scrolls.

Experienced scribes only used Papyrus for hymns, religious texts, letters, official documents, medical texts, scientific manuals, record-keeping and literature. Writing on paper was the most significant way to save and treasure valuable amounts of knowledge from which many modern-day sciences developed

WRITTEN LANGUAGE

According to Wikipedia, English is the most spoken language in the world. But Africa has a rich and long history of writing that predates English and many centuries before colonization. At least nine African writing systems predate the development of Latin, one of the oldest writing systems in Europe.

Egyptian Hieroglyphs
Source ThinkAfrica

Adinkra Alphabet
source pinterest.co.uk

Modern English only started developing in the 17th century AD. English itself is a mixture of French, Latin and Greek, which was brought over by the Anglo Saxons when they invaded the Island. Most European languages are based on Latin, which dates back to 600 BCE.

Egyptian Hieroglyphs are the formal writing system that was used in Ancient Egypt around the 32nd Century BC. The Hieroglyphs were a well-developed language with over 1000 characters distinct from each other. The earliest manuscript is dated from the 28th century BC.

These developed later into forms known as Hieratic dated back to the 32nd century BCE, Demotic between 650 and 400 BCE, Sahidic starts from around 300 AD, The Meroitic script around 2000 BCE etc.,

Apart from Egyptian Hieroglyphs, Africa also had many complex writing systems long before Europeans colonized Africa, and African civilization has had a great culture for thousands of years. This is often ignored, despite the rich African linguistic history appearing centuries before Latin.

Adinkra is a set of symbols developed by the Akan, used to represent concepts and aphorisms. Oral tradition attributes the origin of adinkra to Gyaman in modern-day Ghana and Côte d'Ivoire

EDUCATIONAL INSTITUTIONS

While the west may have entrenched the erroneous belief that Africa was bereft of any form of education and civilization before the arrival of the colonialists, historical evidence has pointed out otherwise. According to history, one of the oldest and first universities in the world was in Timbuktu, Mali. Timbuktu was home to one of the most academic institutions that existed in the early 12th century, The University of Sankoré.

University of Sakore 12th Century
Source one.org

Harvard University 2022
Source hdwalle.com

Ancient books highvelder.co.za

Oxford University Library
Source Medium.com

The university represented the highest level of learning at the time. It had a similar focus to Europe's best Universities, though Sankore University was founded many centuries earlier. The university was renowned for its high standards, producing world-class scholars recognized by their publications. The subjects taught at the University were medicine, surgery, mathematics, physics, astronomy, chemistry, philosophy, language, linguistics, history, geography and art. The University prospered and became a significant intellectual institution, particularly during the 12th to 16th centuries. The university's curriculum has four degrees, and the highest degree level -is equivalent to a PhD. In the 12th century, there was an attendance of about 25,000 students in a city with a population of 100,000. The people of Timbuktu specifically regarded literacy and books as symbols of wealth, power and blessings. In the early 14th century, and by the end of Mansa Musa's reign, the Sankore Mosque had the largest collections of books and manuscripts (between 400,000 to 700,000) in Africa since

This is an excellent departure from the prevailing narrative that Africa was without any education, and that the white European invaders came to civilize Africa. Timbuktu was added to the list of UNESCO world's heritage in 1988.

But even with facts about the place of Timbuktu in history, many still doubt its place in history. In a recent survey of young Brits, a third thought Timbuktu was not a real place and instead, they found the place to be both mystical and imaginary. During the colonial period, tremendous efforts were made to conceal the documents stored in the universities and private libraries. The aforementioned lends credence to the fact that the West misinforms its populace and the world at large of Africa's proper place in the hierarchy of human evolution.

MEDICINE

Medicine is an important field of human knowledge that enriches every society. Breakthroughs in medicine and science have led to increases in the life expectancy of the entire world. The origin of medicine can be traced back to Ancient Africa and Egypt.

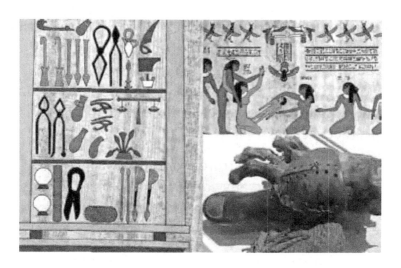

An amputee used this wood and leather prosthetic toe
Source ThinkAfrica.net

Egypt was the first to establish medical schools, such as the Temple of Sais, and develop the practice of specialists evaluating symptoms, treating illnesses through surgery or medicines, and monitoring progress. There was also evidence from written sources –the Ebers Papyrus, the Berlin Papyrus, the Edwin Smith Surgical Papyrus and many others. Some of these documents date back to 2,500 BCE, containing a mixture of innovative thinking and the surgical treatments ancient Egypt mastered. It focuses on bone surgery and external pathology, covering forty-eight cases. Some of the treatments documented in the Smith Papyrus are still used today. The systematic approach of the Smith Papyrus was later transferred to other countries and future generations –to the Near East, Asia, Greek and the Romans.

Among the Niger-Congo civilisations, people facing persistent illness or misfortune turn to a doctor-diviner. Based on studies, 'a witch doctors' in West Africa tended to be men or women knowledgeable about medicines derived from natural sources, the efficacy of those medicines, and people skilled at reading people. Bone-setting was practised by many groups of West Africa, the Akan, Mano, and Yoruba, to name a few.

A lot of knowledge was transferred because of the slave trade from Africans to the Europeans and North America. For example, Kwasi was a slave who was skilled in medical knowledge and treated both slaves and European slave traders. Slaves also discovered the efficacy of many plants and herbs e.g Quinine. Many scientific discoveries came directly as a result of the slave trade. Europeans benefitted economically and scientifically from the slave trade though not Africans were named.

STEEL

Today 1.7 million tonnes of steel are produced each year worldwide. The greatest structures, many gadgets and instruments in today's modern world are made of iron or metal.

In ancient times, the great empires in Africa became great through the fabrication and the usage of high-grade steel to make military weapons made chiefly from iron, such as swords and farming equipment like hoes and cutlass. The Metallurgic sciences have advanced humanity greatly, with metals used for warfare and agriculture. The Edo people of Nigeria were particularly skilled at the manipulation of Brass, and their skills have been immortalised in the famous Benin Bronzes.

Though Benjamin Huntsman was credited with being the English inventor of steel but looking at the historical time proved that this is not the case.

Around 2000 years ago, the Haya people of Tanzania in Africa were the first to invent, make and use steel, with furnaces achieving up to 1500 Celcius. They created their method of smelting iron to produce high-grade steel that was different from those applied by Western nations. To achieve 1300 °C or more temperatures, Tuyere (pipes) were used inside the furnace for preheating. The furnace is called a shaft-bowl type, which means it has a bowl shape. It also is of a forced-air draught type. To run the furnace, the Haya burnt Swamp grass until the bowl was filled with the charred swamp reeds. These reeds provide the carbon which is smelted with the iron to form steel. While the steel produced in this way was not pure steel as we know it today, it was advanced for its time and very great innovation.

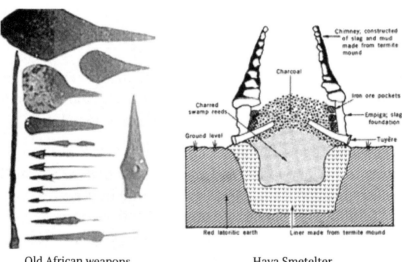

Old African weapons

Haya Smetelter
Source Think Africa.

A recent study managed to reconstruct some of the smelting sites of the Haya Tribe, and the temperature of the furnace reached in excess of 1500 C at the start and throughout the smelting process.

The process at Haya was much more efficient precisely because it avoided producing a bloomery — a type of iron known as sponge iron, which needs to be further refined into pure iron in this step.

GLASS

Glass is an amorphous inorganic solid substance, usually translucent or transparent. Glass is one of the world's oldest and most important man-made materials. Glass affects every part of life; science, industry, work, home, play, and art. So many things, from screens, light bulbs, eye spectacles, thermometers, bottles, fibre optic cables and solar panels. Fibre optic cables are the backbone of the high-speed internet we enjoy today and are a product of glass.

London Glass Skyscraper
Source specfinish.co.uk

Solar panel
source currys.co.uk

Glass is used in construction — for parts such as partitions and windows; in aesthetics; in the automotive and transport industry — for parts such as windscreens, backlights, and mirrors — ; in household products, such as oven doors, TVs, computer screens, smartphones; and a million other products.

The very origins of glass-making can be traced back to Egypt, around 3,500 BC. It was used as a functional and decorative object. During this period, glass-made products were considered precious, and their usage was restricted to the elites. Today, our use of glass has become an essential part of our daily lives. Egypt was primarily responsible for the invention of glass-making and the spread of glass-making techniques to the world's different civilisations.

Ancient Egypt Bead
Source Think AFrica.net

Polychrome glass cup
Source pinterest.com

From 1600 BC, the art of glassmaking began to spread. Around this time, different glass vases of different shapes and sizes were all produced by Egypt. Glass bottle bearing hieroglyphs of Pharaoh Thutmose III is on display at the British Museum.

By 700 BC, alabaster — a form of Egyptian polychromatic vase — was widespread all over the Mediterranean. Around that same time, the art of glass-making was copied by the Phoenicians (present-day Lebanon), who built the glass-making art into a large industry, and from there, the art spread to Cyprus, Greece, and the Italian peninsula. The Phoenicians also discovered how to blow glass with blowing iron sometime around the beginning of the Christian era.

The introduction of man-made glass to society has no doubt been of immense benefit to humans.

ARCHITECTURE

The architecture of Africa is as diverse as the continent itself. African peoples use many building styles that reflect their unique cultures and the different environments in which they live. Africa's buildings and monuments stand as witnesses of Civilization in Africa in the field of Architecture in Ancient Times. Most of Africa's rural peoples use natural materials that are locally available for their buildings. In grasslands, people typically use grasses to cover the walls and roofs of their homes. In forested areas, people build with hardwoods and bamboo and raffia palm. Earth and clay are also major building resources.

Conical tower, Great Zimbabwe's
Souce Tumblr

The Great Mosque of Djenné in Mali
Source aisleseatplease.com

The Great Pyramids of Giza were built in ancient Egypt more than 4,500 years ago and are regarded as one of the greatest architectural feats of all time and are one of the Seven Wonders of the Ancient World. In addition, the conical tower inside the Great Enclosure in Great Zimbabwe, a medieval city built by a prosperous culture, is the largest stone structure South of the Sahara. The site is an architectural marvel, considering how it was all built without using mortar to join the stones. Nubian architecture is one of the most ancient in the world. The architecture includes the speos; structures carved out of solid rock under the A-Group culture (3700-3250 BCE). The Great Mosque of Djenné in Mali, first built in the 13th century, is the largest clay building in the world

MOBILE PHONES

Children mining cobalt in Africa   A child playing with a mobile phone in the UK

You are probably reading this book on your mobile phone, Kindle, or computer. While it may not be obvious to you but the inner workings of your most precious possession lie deep in the soil of the Democratic Republic of Congo in the form of the mineral cobalt, which is used to make your rechargeable batteries.

The Democratic Republic of Congo holds half of the world's cobalt reserves, used to make rechargeable batteries such as those used in mobile phones. The DRC has substantial untapped gold, cobalt and high-grade copper reserves but significant security risks accentuated by a lack of robust infrastructure. In 2019, mine cobalt production in the DRC totalled 100,000 metric tons, accounting for 70 per cent of global production. The DRC was the third largest producer of industrial diamonds in 2019, contributing about 21 per cent of global production.

Tantalum is a shiny, silvery metal that is virtually resistant to corrosion due to an oxide film on its surface. It is used in high-temperature applications, such as aircraft engines; electrical devices, such as capacitors; surgical implants and handling corrosive chemicals.

COTTON

Cotton seed
source etsy.com

Adire cloth
Source adireafricantextiles.com

The author wrote this book section on the hottest summer day since record-keeping began in the United Kingdom. This heat made him appreciate the importance of one of the Ancient African inventions, a comfortable cotton shirt. Cotton is highly sought after because it gets stronger when wet. As a result, the clothing made from them is ideal in the summer, and cotton keeps feet and toes warm and cosy during winter.

According to Hutchinson et al. 1947, cotton was first domesticated about 7,000 years ago. Gossypium herbaceum first appeared in Sudan and Southern Africa, and then it spread into Arabia. The word 'cotton' is derived from the Arabic name "al-qutn".

The cotton fibre was separated from the seed and then carded and spun into yarn before being woven. The yarn or the woven cloth is then dyed. The making of the dye itself was a complex process. There was a time when all these stages were performed by a single family, as in Yorubaland. But as the economy developed, so divided labour. That led to the separation of dyeing from cloth-making and spinning from weaving. Each separation marked greater specialisation and quantitative and qualitative changes in output.

Adire, is a Yoruba (a tribe in Southwestern Nigeria) word for tie and dye. Yoruba women first made it of old by using a variety of resist-dyeing techniques on white colours clothes. The origin of Adire was traced to the archaeological discovery in the Saki area of Oyo state, Nigeria. The first Adire material was made with Teru (local white attire) and Elu (local Dye) made from elu leaf, which grows readily in Saki. Adire patterns are made by pleating the cloth. The colour is kept inside the folds by knotting, dyeing, or stitching with raffia fibre from banana leaves or thread.

LIMITATIONS OF AFRICAN MANUFACTURING

According to Rodney Walter, "the only area where African manufacturers were at a disadvantage was production on a large scale. That is to say, in Africa, the cotton looms were small, the iron smelters were small, the pottery was turned slowly by hand and not on a wheel, etc. This was so because the culture of Africa during this period was one of communalism that focused on each household meeting its own needs by making its clothes, leading to localisation. An exchange was meeting people's needs. This trend was common in African manufacturing during this period, notably in the cloth industry.

African traders and manufacturers also had an element of the guild system. The guild was an association of specialists, passing on their skills by training apprentices and working in buildings set aside for that purpose. For example, there were tailoring guilds at Timbuktu, while Benin guilds of a very restricted caste controlled the famous brass and bronze industry. In Nupe, Nigeria, the glass and bead industries operate on a guild basis. Each Nupe guild had a common workshop and a master. The master obtained contracts, financed the association, and disposed of the product. This amounted to little more than the increasing specialisation and division of labour.

Each community produces surpluses of certain commodities that could be exchanged for items they lack. For example, dried fish is exchanged for yams and millet in a coastal, lake, or riverine area. For small transactions, barter was preferred to some forms of money exchange. It is said that Ghana obtained its gold by "silent" or "mute" barter, a method by which traders who cannot speak each other's language can trade without talking. Group A would leave trade goods in a prominent position and beat great drums to summon the local natives that they had left goods. Group B would then arrive at the spot, examine the goods, and the local natives would then come, place a heap of gold beside each pile, and withdraw. Group A would then return and either accept the trade by taking the goods from Group B or withdraw again, leaving Group B to add to or change items to create an equal value. The transaction ends when Group A accepts Group B's offer and removes the offered goods, leaving Group B to remove the gold and retreat, beating their drums to signify that the market is over.

However, some items were used to measure other goods for complex transactions. For example, salt, cloth, iron hoes, and cowry shells were popular forms of money in Africa.

This page intentionally left blank

7. WHAT THE AFRICAN ANCIENTS KNEW ABOUT FOOD MANUFACTURING

During the history of humanity, there was a point when humans transited from hunting animals and gathering food sources to farming and animal domestication. The transition happens differently in each continent depending on how favourable the environment was to farming, the soil quality, types of available plants, amount of rainfall, climate change etc.

Ancient Africans domesticated and cultivated over 2,000 edible crops for over 3000 years. They include the finger millet, pearl millet, Emmer, Yams, Kolanut, Coffee and Sorghum.

Africa's ability to be food sufficient is ever more critical, especially now that the current war in Ukraine and Russia. This war, many miles away from Africa, is causing the cost of bread, grains and other foodstuffs to skyrocket to an all-time high. It is important to note that our Africans' ancestors have domesticated crops that would pave the road for future generations to live sufficiently depending on their agricultural products rather than spending billions on food. Money that could be spent on developing Africa's societies.

Humanity has not fully exploited the complete variety of foods domesticated by Africa because it is among the least researched continents on earth. In some circles, there is a belief that food domesticated in Africa is either inferior, less nutritious or less beneficial to humankind. In this section, we will look at some of Africa's contributions and the diversity they added to humanity's food supply.

KOLA NUT

Kolanut
source healthcautions.com

Pepsi and Cola
Source patheos.com

Coca-Cola is the most recognizable beverage brand in the world, followed by Pepsi Cola. Although much of the western society will credit pharmacist John Pemberton for inventing Coke in 1886 and pharmacist Caleb Bradham for inventing Pepsi, the inspiration for Coke and Pepsi lies in the domestication of the Kola nut by ancient West Africans 7,000 years ago. Kola nut was and still is a fruit with sacred and social significance to West Africans.

Kola nut is a wonder fruit that has its origin in the tropical rainforest region of Africa, and they are extracted from the evergreen kola tree. These nuts are super rich in caffeine and are linked with several health benefits. They are somewhat bitter when chewed in the mouth. Kola nut also has many uses; it is chewed during special events in certain African countries. It can be used to sweeten the breath and serves as a flavouring agent for sodas and as an additive in energy drinks and performance enhancers.

The Coca-Cola Company, which manufactures soft drinks, employs 61,800 people and generates annual sales of 35 billion US dollars annually. The love of Coke around the world demonstrates that Africa has a lot to offer the world.

PALM OIL

Palm tree
Source ledgerinsights.com

Palm oil processing
Source grain.org

Palm oil production is one African product that is impossible to go through a day without using it several times. For example, if you have used personal care products today, such as shampoo and toothpaste or used household cleaning products such as detergents and cleansers, you have used Palm oil. Palm oil is found in almost 50% of food products in the supermarket, requiring a fat component such as chocolates to biscuits and peanut butter to ice cream, palm oil in its various forms and derivatives is a common ingredient in these food products.

The oil palm (Elaeis guineensis) originated from West Africa, where evidence of its use as a staple food crop dates back as 5,000 years. In the late 1800s, archaeologists discovered a substance they concluded was originally palm oil in a tomb at Abydos dating back to 3,000 BCE, reflecting the high societal value attributed to the product. With origins in West Africa and evidence of consumption in Egypt, palm oil can be considered one of the earliest traded commodities.

Palm oil is an edible vegetable oil derived from the mesocarp (reddish pulp) of the fruit of the oil palms. Oil is used in food manufacturing, beauty products, and biofuel. Palm oil accounted for about 33% of global oils produced from oil crops in 2014. Palm oils are easier to stabilize and maintain quality of flavour and consistency in processed foods, so food manufacturers frequently favour them. On average, globally, humans consume 7.7 kg (17 lb) of palm oil per person.

Palm oil became a highly sought-after commodity by British traders for use as an industrial lubricant for machinery during Britain's Industrial Revolution. Palm oil formed the basis of soap products, such as Lever Brothers' (now Unilever) "Sunlight" soap and the American Palmolive brand. By around 1870, palm oil constituted the primary export of some West African countries, although this was overtaken by cocoa in the 1880s with the introduction of colonial European cocoa plantations.

COFFEE

There is a high chance that you will probably prepare or buy coffee when you wake up this morning or on your way to work. You might have bought your filtered coffee with or without sugar, syrups or whipped cream from one of the coffee and snack shops. But have you ever wondered about the origin of this favourite stimulant?

Archaeologists traced the ancient coffee forests of Ethiopia back to the 10th century. According to local history, coffee was accidentally discovered by a local goat herder called Kaldi. Kaldi noticed that when his goats eat certain berries from a tree, they become so energetic that they wouldn't even sleep at night. Kaldi told the abbot of the local monastery about the unusual berries he found. The abbot tried the berries out for himself and turned them into a drink. He discovered that the berries-based drink did help him to stay alert during evening prayer. He shared this information about the berries with other monks at the monastery. From there on, the story of the miracle berries that would provide amazing energy levels began.

Coffee bean Source mashed.com

Coffee is now the most popular drink worldwide. Coffee and snacks shop is an industry worth more than $30 billion annually, with around two billion cups consumed daily. 64% of American adults currently consume coffee every day. More than 150 million Americans drink about 400 million cups of coffee daily. An average American drinks 3.1 cups of coffee daily, which is more than 140 billion cups per year.

Next time you visit Starbuck or Costa Coffee, always remember Kaldi, the goat herder in Ethiopia who discovered coffee berries

SHEA BUTTER

Shea butter
Source supermelanin.co.za

Shea butter is a fat extracted from the nut of the African shea tree (Vitellaria paradoxa). When raw, it is ivory in colour and commonly dyed yellow with palm oil. It is widely used in cosmetics as a moisturizer, salve or lotion. Shea butter is rich in vitamins A and E, which help balance, moisturise and soothe skin, and vitamin F, which helps revitalise damaged hair and skin. Shea butter is edible and is used in food preparation in some African countries.

The shea tree grows naturally in the wild in the d

ry savannah belt of West Africa from Senegal to Sudan in the east and in 21 countries across the African continent.

Cleopatra became queen of Egypt in 51 BC. She is one of the best-known women in history, famed for her beauty and intellect. History tells us that caravans of clay jars filled with shea butter were brought to her in Egypt for use. Shea butter has been a beauty secret for queens.

The English word "shea" comes from sǐ, the tree's name in Bambara. It is known by many local names, such as nkuto in Twi, kaɗe or kaɗanya in Hausa, òkwùmá in the Igbo language, òrí in the Yoruba language and in some parts of West Africa and many others. It is used in the cosmetic industry for soap, lip balm, skin lotion or even shaving cream that contains shea butter.

AFRICAN RICE

African Rice
Source .vanguardngr.com

You cannot have any African ceremony without serving your guest rice. In some African countries, rice symbolizes fertility, luck and wealth. Rice is the most widely consumed staple food for an enormous part of the world's population, especially in Africa and Asia. Its agricultural production takes third place worldwide (741.5 million tonnes), after sugarcane (1.9 billion tonnes) and maize (1.0 billion tonnes). Rice is an important grain because humans solely consume it, providing more than one-fifth of the calories consumed worldwide.

Grain rice is a seed of either *Oryza glaberrima* (African rice) or *Oryza sativa* (Asian rice). The Mande people domesticated and cultivated African rice between 3,500 BC and 1,500 BC. It spread from its original centre in the Niger River delta and extended to Senegal, and African rice was preferred for its taste. Farmers would grow African rice for consumption, and they grew Asian rice to sell.

African rice has more excellent resistance to many biotic and abiotic stresses than Asian rice and can compete with weeds. It also requires low labour and is suited to various harsh conditions. However, the higher levels of grain breakage during milling– due to the prevailing hot and dry conditions in the sub Sahara regions during the harvest season — and the red pericarp made it not appealing to the international market. However, it has been proven that red pericarp rice possesses superior nutritional qualities, and thus, its use should be encouraged.

Africa currently imports a total of about $5.6 billion worth of rice. This is shocking because Africa's ancestors domesticated a crop that would pave the road for future generations to live sufficiently depending on their agricultural products rather than having to spend billions on food that could be spent on developing Africa's societies. The African rice seeds were carried as supplies on slave ships, and the African enslaved rice farmers were the ones who brought about the technology and skills needed for the rice plant to grow in America.

YAM

Yam is an intricate part of the culture of some societies in West Africa, as rice was to certain societies in Asia. Yam is the common name for the starchy vegetable root tubers of the Dioscorea genus family. The yam tubers come in different shapes and sizes, can weigh up to 40 kg and are as long as 4 feet long. It usually has rough skin with colour that ranges from white, yellow, and purple to dark brown.

Yam
Source ThinkAfrica.net

Yams grow typically in tropical climates with moderate to high rainfall. According to Washington International Food Policy Research Institute (IFPRI) West Africa accounts for 96% of the world's total yam production. Out of which Nigeria contributes a whopping 66%, and around 50 million tonnes, followed by Ghana (8 million tonnes) and Ivory Coast (7 million tonnes).

The agricultural cultivation of yam was first practised as early as 5000BC in West Africa. The White yam was domesticated by African farmers that discovered it growing wild in the forest-savannah region of the eastern part of West Africa, in south-eastern Nigeria, home of the Igbo people. It was preferred because of its good taste and superior nutritional benefits. A typical yam is cylindrical with rough dark brown skin and white inner flesh.

Though the yam thrives well in Guinea Savannah and humid forest regions of Africa, the Igbo people are reputed to have the most advanced yam culture and sophistication globally. However, there was also wide-scale domestication and cultivation of this crop by the Yorubas, Igbos, Efiks, Tivs, and other smaller ethnic minorities.

There is a popular proverb in the Igbo language that states "önye ume ngwu anaghi ako Ji" which translates to "a lazy person cannot cultivate yam". Yam cultivation is an exacting process, tedious and labour intensive. The lengthy and arduous task of cultivating yams takes about seven months of activity. The cultivation includes clearing the land, tillage, readying and preparing the yam setts and tubers for planting, staking and trailing the yam vines, weeding, harvesting, readying the yam barns and tying the yam tubers to the barn racks. Families that accomplish these tasks convey the status of wealth and privilege. The difficulty associated with yam cultivation adds to its value in the region as a social, economic and cultural crop for strong and serious-minded individuals and a symbol of social status and authority.

The Importance of this crop in West Africa cannot be overemphasized. The White yam, for instance, when all of its resources are fully exploited yam can feed a community for a whole year, and many ethnic groups from the region are aware and have taken full advantage of this. In Nigeria, a very popular local delicacy known as Amala is produced from dried-out pieces of yam that have been ground into powder and added to boiling water to form a thick paste which is then consumed with various local soups and sauces.

For the Igbo ethnic group in south-east Nigeria, yam is the most popular and favourite food. It plays a significant role in marriage ceremonies, thanksgiving ceremonies, burials, and traditional rituals. In some cultures, a man's wealth is determined by the quantity of yam he has stored in his barn.

In China, Korea, and Japan, for instance, Yam is used for traditional medicine and also used to make ice creams and the popular wagashi cakes in Japan. The mucilaginous tuber milk contains allantoin, a cell-proliferate which when applied to abscesses, ulcers, and boils, speeds up healing.

SORGHUM

A variety of Sorghum called sorghum bicolour originated in Burundi. Sorghum is 11,000-year-old domestication that became the 5th most important crop. Sorghum is the world's fifth most important cereal crop, after rice, wheat, maize and barley.

The name "sorghum" is derived from the Italian word "sorgo", which is a modification of the Latin "Syricum (granum)", which means "grain of Syria". Sorghum bicolour is a globally important crop with many uses: as food in the form of popcorn, flatbread, sorghum grain, sorghum molasses; production of alcoholic beverages, biofuels and animal fodder. Sorghum is heat-tolerant, drought-resistant and cheap to produce or buy for poor people.

It is grown extensively in warmer areas, mainly in Africa and southern and western Asia. It has long been the staple food of millions of people in these areas owing to its high protein content (9%), the genius of pre-historic Africans and its ability to grow in very harsh conditions.

Sorghum
Source dekalbasgrowdeltapine.com

However, despite being one of the most vastly cultivated crops, developed early in farming and arguably originating before even rice, the history of Sorghum is relatively obscure. Recently, sorghum has been appreciated as a healthy alternative to wheat for a lot of diets. Sorghum is a gluten-free staple grain for individuals with celiac disease and other gluten intolerances, and it is also the ideal grain for people with diabetes.

Sorghum also has high nutritional value, with high levels of unsaturated fats, protein, fibre, and minerals like phosphorus, potassium, calcium, and iron. It also has more antioxidants than blueberries and pomegranates.

Africa has been blessed with the perfect climate to grow sorghum, with the recent high rise in the cost of grains. Africa is positioned to provide the majority of the world's rising demand for sorghum as Asia did with Rice production. Since 2005, sorghum production has risen by nearly 66% worldwide, making it a very lucrative opportunity for growth. Focusing on cultivating sorghum will make Africa self-sufficient in food and provide levers to develop into a global net exporter rather than a net importer.

OTHER CROPS

COWPEA (Vigna unguiculata): Black eye pea is native to central Africa, one of Africa's most popular grain legumes, and its seeds are precious human food. It contains a high amount of protein.

EGGPLANT (Solanum aethiopicum): is a fruiting plant found in the tropical areas of Africa. Its leaves and fruit can be eaten raw or cooked. The Igbo people of Nigeria use it as a substitute for kola nut in rituals and events.

EGUSI (Citrullus lanatus): It looks like a small round watermelon. It is a major source of soup ingredients and the daily meal for most of its population in West Africa, where soups are integral to life.

LOCUST BEAN (Parkia biglobosa): This is a multi-purpose legume tree found in tropical African countries. It is called iru or ogiri okpei by the Yoruba and Igbo people of Nigeria, respectively. Its seeds, fruit and leaves are used in the preparation of many foods and drinks.

GROUNDNUT: Groundnut, monkey nut or peanut are often used interchangeably. Groundnuts and groundnut-based products can be marketed as nutritional foods to combat energy, protein, and micronutrient malnutrition among the needy, as they are highly nutritious. India, China, Myanmar, and Vietnam heavily use groundnut oil for cooking purposes. The most popular groundnut food in the USA, Canada, and Australia is peanut butter. Groundnut seeds can be eaten raw (non-heat-ed), boiled, and fried, and can also be used to produce baked goods with confectionery and flour.

JOLLOF RICE

Jollof Rice
Source cookpad.com

If you ever go out to an African restaurant outside the continent, there is a high chance that you will be offered Jollof Rice. Jollof rice is a rice dish from West Africa. The dish is typically made with long-grain rice, tomatoes, onions, spices, vegetables and meat in a single pot, with slight variation in ingredients and preparation methods varying across different West African regions.

Jollof rice is becoming so popular in England that a well-known TV chef Jamie Oliver has written a recipe for Jollof Rice.

The origins of jollof rice can be traced to the Senegambian region that was ruled by the Wolof or Jolof Empire in the 14th century, spanning parts of today's Senegal, The Gambia and Mauritania, where rice was grown. The dish has its roots in a traditional dish called thieboudienne, containing rice, fish, shellfish and vegetables.

Since the 2010s, there has been increasing interest in West African foods in the western world. Jollof food festivals have been held in Washington, DC, US, and Toronto, Canada. "World Jollof Day" has been celebrated since 2015 on 22 August, gaining traction on social media.

This page intentionally left blank

8. INTERNATIONAL TRADE IN ANCIENT AFRICA BEFORE SLAVERY

We have spent the last few chapters correcting the erroneous teaching that the ancient Africans had little or nothing to do with the development and progression of civilization. The massive number of anthropological sources proved that the origins of several advancements hailed from Africa and that many essential things we utilize today should be rightfully credited to the ancient accomplishments of Africa's ancient civilizations.

Though the earliest fossil of humans was found in East Africa about 2.8 million years ago, anthropologists have found signs of primitive life in other parts of Africa. These findings suggest that humanity's origin is not restricted to East Africa alone but rather the entire continent of Africa.

This section will consider other areas of Africa where civilisation existed long before civilisation started in other parts of the world. We will look at examples of development in early Africa, in areas such as Egypt, Ethiopia, Nubia, Morocco, Western Sudan, and Zimbabwe, to give a snippet of Africa's economy and civilisation.

THE EGYPTIAN EMPIRE

Egypt parade
Source gulfnews.com

Egypt was the oldest African culture, which rose to eminence and was the first recorded monarch in human history. Egyptologists agreed that ancient Egypt started around 4,500 BC. The ancient Africans built the city of Memphis in ancient Egypt in 3100 B.C. this was nearly 2000 years before any European civilisation. The Greeks built Athens in 1200 B.C., and the Romans built Rome in 1000 B.C.

The early Egyptian civilization had to invent things from scratch because they were the pioneer of many discoveries. They were the first to discover metallurgy, astronomy, writing, paper, medicine, mechanics & machinery (including ramps, levers, ploughs and mills) and all that goes for the continuation of a large organized society. Their exploration of the different fields of studies allowed them to create iconic inventions such as the pyramids, the first codified form of writing (hieroglyphics), the papyrus sheets, black ink, the calendar, and the clock name a few.

Africa's oldest known writing system dates back to over 6000 years ago. While on the other hand, Europe's oldest writing dates back to 1400 BC, which was used by the Greeks yet largely derived from the Proto-Sinaitic, an old African script. The most famous indigenous writing system emerged from Africa is the Egyptian hieroglyphs, which later developed into Hieratic, Demotic and Coptic.

Hieroglyphs from Egypt
Source gulfnews.com

The writing material of the medieval times, known as the papyrus, was derived from the aquatic plant *Cyperus papyrus*, which was native to the Nile delta region in Egypt. Many papyri survive to date, telling us of ancient discoveries by the Egyptians. Among those is the ancient Egyptian dating system or the first calendar that used a year of 365 days.

THE KINGDOM OF AXUM WAS AROUND ETHIOPIA

Obelisk of Axum
Source .pinterest.co.uk

Axum was founded near the Red Sea coast from 100 AD to 940 AD. The city of Aksum is the seventh oldest continuously inhabited city in Africa, with the first signs of human inhabitancy dating back to 400 BC. The Empire of Axum, at times, extended across most of present-day Eritrea, northern Ethiopia, Western Yemen, and parts of eastern Sudan. The capital city of the empire was Axum, now in northern Ethiopia. The Emperor of Ethiopia was addressed as 'Conquering Lion of the Tribe of Judah, Elect of God, King of Kings'. It has been proven that the 'Solomonic' line of this tribe from the Queen of Sheba in the Bible was not unbroken to date in Ethiopia. The biblical accounts of this royal meeting are found in the Bible, 1st Kings and 2nd Chronicles 2. The story was portrayed as a monarchical meeting on state affairs with no hint of romance to the encounter. However, the book Song of Solomon referred to the love between King Solomon and the Queen of Sheba.

The Obelisk of Axum is 24 metres tall (79-feet high), made of granite, weighs 160 tonnes and dates from the 4th century. The Church of Our Lady Mary of Zion has been destroyed and rebuilt several times. It was originally constructed in the 4th century by the Ethiopian Orthodox Church, believed to be during the reign of King Ezana, the first Christian ruler of Axum, and claims to contain the Ark of the Covenant. It is located in Tigray, Ethiopia.

The architectural achievements in the Kingdom of Axum attest to the level of skill reached by Ethiopians and the state's capacity to mobilise labour on a huge scale. In the 6th century A.D,

THE KINGDOM OF NUBIA

This is a region along the Nile river in present-day Sudan. Nubia was another African region regarded as the Land of Great Natural Wealth and the world's envy. Scholars were fascinated by the ruins of large red-brick churches and monasteries, which had murals and frescoes of fine quality. Skilled labour was involved in making the bricks, the painting, and the architecture. The military organization centred on archery as the infantry was mostly equipped with swords, axes, clubs and shields. Weapons during this period were made of bronze. Dozens of royal tombs he uncovered there date to between 1750 and 1500 B.C.

Nubia and Egypt date far back into history in terms of relating against each other than in alliances. They had conquered themselves times without number due to various pretexts. A major reason for Egypt's conquering of Nubia was the Nile River.

Fortifications unearthed by Archaeologist Bonnet et al. showed that around 2500 B.C., the people of Kerma constructed a large fortress. The Nubian fortifications were nearly always built in mud-brick. The specification was 37×18×12cm (15×7×5 in). The rising wall of the fortress was covered with white plaster and regarded as one of the oldest military installations. The complexity of its design poses a challenge to views that Africa did not produce military innovations that influenced and set the bar for other civilisations when Aniba was built.

An aerial view of the city of Dukki Gel
Source Sudanese Archaeological Mission of Kerma

BENIN EMPIRE AND THE GREAT WALLS OF BENIN

The Great precolonial Benin kingdom is one of the oldest West African civilisations in existence from 355 BC to the present. The kingdom is recognised for its brilliant bronze, ivory, iron artefacts and military prowess.

The old Benin city is still the present-day location of Benin city in Edo state, South-west Nigeria. When the Europeans first arrived at the Benin kingdom in the late 15th Century, they were astonished by the wealth, quality of life and organization. This was at a time when London was

A Benin Bronze plaque in   Aerial of Benin city (British Museum)
the British Museum

The Dutch writer Olfert Dapper wrote the following in Dutch and translated it into English, an account of merchants who had seen Benin:

"Benin City is at least four miles wide. The city has wide, straight roads lined by houses. The houses are large and handsome, with walls made from clay. The people are very friendly, and there seems to be no stealing.

Inside the city is the king's court. It is large and square and surrounded by a wall. The court is divided into many palaces with separate houses and apartments for courtiers.

The court has many galleries flanked by wooden pillars. Fixed to these pillars are shining metal plaques showing battle scenes and deeds of courage. The palace roofs have pointed turrets; a copper bird without spread wings is on top of each turret.

The king shows himself to his people just once a year, riding horseback out of his court. He is beautifully dressed with all sorts

of royal ornaments. Three or four hundred noblemen accompany their king, some on horseback and some on foot. And a great number of musicians walk before and behind him, playing merry tunes on all sorts of musical instruments.

The king doesn't ride very far from the court but soon returns after a little tour. Then he orders some tame leopards that he keeps to be led about the city in chains."

The first set of Portuguese that came to Benin was astonished at this paradise in the middle of the African jungle made up of hundreds of interlocked cities and villages; they named it The Great City of Benin. This was a period when there was hardly any other place in Africa the Europeans acknowledged as a city.

According to a Portuguese ship captain Lourenco Pinto in 1691, *"Benin was larger than Lisbon, wealthy, industrious and well-governed to the extent that there was no theft. He observed that the level of security was such that the people had no doors in their houses".*

Houses and streets were highly organized in a mathematical pattern unknown to Europeans at the time. Initially, they thought it was disorganized, and the streets were very broad and ran straight as further as the eye could see. Benin was one of the first ancient cities to have some kind of street light. These were huge metal lamps placed around the city with a wick fuelled by palm oil to illuminate at night.

Massive walls and deep ditches surrounded Benin city, which stretched beyond the city walls. Numerous other walls, moats, and ramparts separated its surroundings into about 500 settlements.

This massive fortification was the lengthiest in the world and was constructed by the Edo people of the Great Kingdom of

Benin. This ancient wonder was on par with world wonders like the Taj Mahal of India or the Great Wall of China. It was constructed to secure and protect the kingdom from invaders.

Work on the fortification first began around 800 AD and continued up until around 1460. The structure, upon completion, comprised of ditches and ramparts, covered a border distance of about 16,000 kilometres, 16,000 sq. kilometres and enclosed about 6,500 square kilometres of community land in an assortment of more than 500 interconnected villages. Altogether this was double the length of the Ming Great Wall of China, which measured 8,851 kilometres. The new official length of 21,196 kilometres was announced on June 5th 2012, after the discovery of the Walls of Benin displaced the Great Wall of China under its old measurements.

The Great Wall of China in 2010 attracted approximate 24 million people and generated about $3 billion in revenue. On the other hand, the Benin walls had no such opportunity because huge sections of the walls were destroyed during the British punitive expedition. In present-day Benin, ruins of this grand structure remain scattered all over Edo Lands, and locals use them as a source for obtaining building resources while real estate developers gradually tear down some parts of it. Today sadly, barely any trace of this structural phenomenon exists.

One can only imagine if this magnificent relic from such a rich history were in places like England, USA, Germany, or even India. It would have been the most visited place in the world, a tourist haven for millions worldwide, and a money spinner for Nigeria generating billions in annual tourist revenue.

The British Punitive Expedition in the Palace of the Oba of Benin 1897.

The kingdom quickly established trade relations with the Europeans, and soon word began to spread around Europe of the magnificent kingdom in the African forests. Trouble started in the 19th century due to increased European interference, and great Britain sought control over the kingdom's rich resources and trade. Hostilities kept rising and ultimately climaxed to the destruction and looting of the Kingdom in 1897 by the British with their superior firepower, in a retaliatory attack after eight members of a British entourage were killed by Benin warriors.

THE ASANTE KINGDOM

The Western Sudanic empires of Ghana, Mali and Songhai demonstrated the achievements of the African past. They proved that Africans, too, were capable of political, administrative and military greatness in the epoch before the white men.

The old Ghana Empire   Ashanti talking drum

The Ashanti kingdom was formed from a coalition of Ashanti clans and large city-states in 750 AD. The kingdom covered 250,000 square kilometres and ruled a population of 3 million. In comparison, during the same period, the United Kingdom covered 242,000 square kilometres and had a population of 10 million.

The Ashanti used the talking drum to communicate distances of 300 kilometres or at nearly the same speeds as the telegraph. The messages sent by the drums broadcasted announcements, warned of potential danger, and were used to call meetings. The language of the state was Twi, a tonal language. The Ashanti had road networks, transport and communication systems. The Ashanti army numbered close to 200,000 people, making it larger than the Zulu army and as big as some of the armies in Ethiopia.

The Ashanti captured Mauritania and Mali, where they founded the Ghana empire lasting from 750 AD until 1,200 AD. The tradition of the Ghana empire refers to a founder called Dingha Cisse, a man "from the east". The name Ghana means "warrior king" in Soninke, a language from the region of the empire of Ghana.

The empire of Ghana grew and traded in salt, kola nuts, gold and ivory. The rule of law in the Ashanti Kingdom was based on religious rules, and they believed that crime was a sin that disrespected the ancestors and should be punished. The head of the Ashanti was called the Asantehene, and he was the only one who could invoke a death sentence and was the Army's Supreme Commander.

The decline of the empire of Ghana started during the spread of Islam to the empire. Islam came with lots of violence as some of his subjects began to identify as Muslim above nationality. The switch in religion eroded the authority of the king of Ghana, and eventually, another dynasty was able to subdue Ghana and annex its goldfields, the source of its wealth.

THE ANGLO-ASANTE WARS

Britain gained a foothold in West Africa first through piracy and in-land slave raids during the 16th century by Sir John Hawkins and then established a navy and forts on the Gold Coast in the 19th century. The British fought a total of four wars against the Ashanti Kingdom over almost a century before finally incorporating it into the Gold Coast Colony. Despite the strength of the British Navy during this period, the brave Ashanti warriors were able to hold them off their land for a century.

The Asante Wars were a series of four battles between the Asante and the British. The Asante won the first war lasting eight years between 1823 and 1831. Later in 1834, Britain outlawed slavery, and these diplomatic efforts dealt a major blow to the Asante Kingdom, whose coastline was used to sell 10,000 slaves a year. Britain also fueled instability in the region by siding with vassal states of the Ashantiland — Denkyira and the Fante Federation — to wage wars against the Ashante. The second war against the Asante was a draw during 1863-1864. The third battle was settled with a peace treaty in 1874. A fourth war violated this peace treaty in 1894-1896 that Britain won, turning Ashanti-land into part of the Gold Coast protectorate of Britain. After defeating the Asante, Britain sent the Asantehene into exile in Seychelles.

YAA ASANTEWAA AND THE WAR OF THE GOLDEN STOOL

Already humiliated and defeated, the British administrator of the Gold Coast Sir Frederick Mitchell went to Kumasi, the capital of the Asante Kingdom and demanded to sit on the Golden Stool. The Golden Stool was a religious symbol and in the Asante Kingdom, no commoner, no foreigner, no aristocrat other than the Asantehene could sit on the Golden Stool. Enraged at inaction by the men present at that time, Yaa Asantewaa, the queen mother of the Ashanti kingdom, made a speech which sparked the War of the Golden Stool with British. After several engagements, 1,000 deaths on the British side with Sir Frederick Mitchell Hodgson along with his retinue rescued at the last minute.

What is remarkable is that a woman, a Queen Mother Yaa As-antewaa in her sixties led a war to protect the dignity of her people and won against British representatives armed with Maxim guns. She was eventually send to exile and managed to live 21 more years and died 81.

MALI EMPIRE

Mansa Musa, ruler of Mali in the 1300s
IMAGE ILLUSTRATION BY TIM O'BRIEN

The Mali Empire was an empire in West Africa from c. 1235 to 1670. The empire was founded by Sundiata Keita (c. 1214 — c. 1255). The Mali Empire was once one of Africa's largest, richest, and most powerful empires.

Mali empire in the 1300s was the size of western Europe alone, and it went from the Atlantic coast to the Niger river and included many of the western Sahara desert trade towns. Unknown to many in the developed world, Mali was a centre of civilisation, and Timbuktu University was the first university in the world. The kingdom lasted for centuries and had a lasting effect on Africa and beyond.

The city of Timbuktu (present-day Mali) in the 14th century was five times bigger than the city of London. It was the wealthiest city in the world and had the richest man in the history of humanity. At the time of his death in 1331, Mansa Musa was worth the equivalent of 400 billion dollars (twice the worth of Jeff Bezos' net worth of $213.11 billion in 2021). At that time, the Mali Empire was producing more than half the world's supply of salt and gold. When Mansa Musa went on a pilgrimage to Mecca in 1324, he carried so much gold and spent it so lavishly that the price of gold fell for ten years. Sixty thousand people accompanied him. He founded the library of Timbuktu and the famous manuscripts of Timbuktu, which cover all areas of world knowledge.

National Geographic recently described Timbuktu as the Paris of the Medieval World on account of its intellectual culture. According to Professor Henry Louis Gates, 25,000 university students studied there. When these events were happening in Africa, Europe as a continent was plunged into the Dark Ages. Europe was ravaged by plague, famine, and the killing of people for religious and ethnic reasons.

Mali reigned in the 13th and 14th centuries, and Songhai in the two subsequent centuries. Though these three empires are often referred to as trading states, the main occupation of the citizens of these empires was agriculture. These areas saw the relatively early introduction of iron in the millennium before the birth of Christ, and iron tools exerted their attendant benefits on agriculture.

Cotton cultivation led to the making of cotton cloth with a variety of specialisations that there was international trade in particular cotton cloths, such as the unbleached fabric of Futa Jalon and the blue cloth of Jenne. Pastoralism provided various products for manufacture, notably cattle hides and goat-skins, which went into the making of sandals, leather jackets for military use, leather pouches for amulets, and so on. Horses served as a means of transport for the ruling class and contributed significantly to warfare and the size of the state.

On the edge of the Sahara, the camel took over another "technological" asset introduced from the north. Mining was one sphere in which production was important. The merchants who came from the great cities of Western Sudan had to buy the gold by weight, using a small, accurate measurement known as the Benda. When the Portuguese arrived at the river Gambia in the 1450s and saw how gold was traded in the river's upper reaches, they marvelled at the dexterity of the Mandinga merchants.

THE ASTRONOMICAL KNOWLEDGE OF THE DOGON TRIBE OF MALI DATES BACK TO 3200 BC

The Dogon people are renowned for their knowledge of the Sirius system, dating back to 3200 BC before scientists discovered it in 1862. They are also best known for their religious traditions, mask dances, wooden sculpture, and architecture.

French anthropologist Marcel Griaule has claimed that Dogon's traditional religion incorporates details about extrasolar astronomical bodies that could not have been discerned from naked-eye observation. The scientist reported that the Dogon believes that Sirius A, the brightest star in Earth's night sky, had a much dimmer companion: Sirius B, Digitaria star. When Digitaria is closest to Sirius, that star brightens: when it is farthest from Sirius, it gives off a sparkling effect that suggests to the observer several stars. The orbit cycle takes 50 years. They also claimed that the Dogon knew of the rings of Saturn and the moons of Jupiter.

However, since the last Sigui celebration was in 1967, the next celebration is expected to happen in 2027. They believe that the celebration of Sirius B's rotation comes to renew the earth.

KINGDOM OF ZIMBABWE (1220-1450 AD)

The word Zimbabwe is loosely translated to 'House of Rock'. The first inhabitants settled in this area as early as the 5th century AD, according to some pottery shards found in this area. These were the Shona people, who originated from Southern Africa and migrated towards the north.

The Kingdom of Zimbabwe controlled the ivory and gold trade from the interior to the southeastern coast of Africa.

One of the significant constructions in Zimbabwe is brick (dated around the 14th century). The Zimbabwean people built mainly with stone and mud. They had perfected the technique of cutting and shaping the stone in such a way that the stones could be stacked in a wall perfectly without the use of mortar, and the wall would hold its shape and integrity. This technique was used extensively in the city of Great Zimbabwe, mainly on the walls. There are two significant walls in the city. One outer wall protected the main city from invaders, and one inner wall divided the city into two parts. The building in the inner area was constructed with granite and stone, cut to perfection and stacked with one another.

One European archaeologist said that "there was as much labour expended in Zimbabwe as on the Pyramids in Egypt". Skill, creativity and artistry went into the construction of the walls, especially concerning the decorations, the inner recesses and the doors.

House of stone
Souce Tumblre

Zimbabwe was a mixed farming zone, with cattle being important since the area is free from tsetse flies. Irrigation and terracing reached considerable proportions. Small streams were diverted and made to flow around hills, indicating an awareness of the scientific principles governing water motion.

OYO EMPIRE

Oyo Empire is a West African monarchy that, at its peak, covered 270,000 square kilometres. The Oyo Empire was a powerful Yoruba state in what is now western Nigeria. It began in the 1300s in the West African savannah north of the tropical forests where other Yoruba peoples lived. Being in the savannah proved beneficial, as Oyo could use horses obtained from Europe and North Africa for the cavalry. Using armoured cavalry, the empire was able to extend its reach across parts of what is now northern and western Nigeria.

The empire grew during the eighteenth century as it became more involved in slave trading. Oyo also maintained its traditional position as brokers and traders between Yorubas to the south and Hausas to the north.

Oyo Brass wikimedia.org

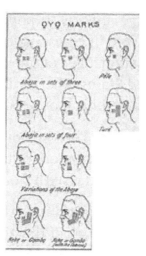

Oyo tribal mark

In the late eighteenth century, the empire came to rely too much on slave sales to Europeans—when the trade declined and eventually ended, Oyo suffered. As the state's income and authority declined, some of its subjects began to rebel. This allowed weaker peripheral states to break free of Oyo's control. One of those states, Dahomey, soon became a political and military rival in the southwest. Oyo was also affected by the Fulani Jihad waged by Muslims on its northern frontier. Eventually, these provinces broke free as well.

The Oyo Kingdom was ruled by a monarch, till today, called the *Alaafin*, who a Council advised of seven officials called the *Oyo Mesi*. The Oyo Mesi had the power to elect each new king by drawing from the pool of people with Royal lineage and also the power to make the *Alaafin* commit suicide if deemed unfit to rule the people.

The legitimacy of the Oyo monarchy traces back to a mythical hero of the Yoruba people called *Oduduwa*, also called *Oodua*.

During the colonial period, the Yorubas were one of the most urbanized groups in Africa. About 22% of the population lived in large areas with populations exceeding 100,000, and over 50% lived in cities made up of 25,000 or more people. The urbanisation index of the Yorubas in 1950 was close to that of the United States. The Yoruba continue to be the most urbanized African ethnic group today.

Bronze art. The kingdom of Oyo is a brainchild of the same civilisation that produce the Ife Bronze sculptures. The founder of Oyo was the sixth Ooni of Ife.

National Historians. Although Yoruba was not a written language for much of the history of Oyo, there were national historians, the King's drummers, cymbalists and bards whose job was to remember Yoruba history through oral tradition, poetry and musical devices. The kingdom of Oyo had a standing army and a reserve army (drawn from the tributaries). The head of the army was the "Aare Ona Kakanfo".

Loans — The Yoruba developed various systems of advancing personal loans, despite the absence of writing, such as the iwo-fa system.

Oriki — Oriki is praise poetry, and there is no prescribed length for praise poetry. Traditionally, each child would have praise poetry, each kingship line, and each province, capturing their historical achievements or reputation within Yorubaland.

Facial recognition. The people of Yoruba land used facial scarification to mark the province of origin of their citizens (Town Identification). The naming system then indicated the family or social rank, lineage, seniority, or circumstance of birth. The tribal marks allow Yorubas to trace themselves and link town and family members thousands of miles from home during slavery.

In conclusion, we started this chapter by examining ancient Africans' knowledge before encountering Europe. We also consider the political and economic situation of a few places in Africa to convince readers that Africa before the 15th century was not just a jumble of different tribes. Like other continents, most African societies started with communalism and slowly evolved toward a feudal state. Before African contact with Europeans, agriculture was the overwhelmingly dominant activity in Africa. Despite the crudeness and the simplicity of the tools used for farming, the farmers were very good at it, and agriculture was very productive.

This page intentionally left blank

9. THE AFRICAN DIASPORA CONTRIBUTION TO MODERN CIVILISATION

According to historian Patrick Manning, despite the dark history of black people through slavery and colonialism, blacks have laboured day and night at the centre of forces that created the modern world. This finding contradicts the traditional Eurocentric perspective that has dominated history books, presenting Africans and diasporans as primitive victims of slavery without historical agency.

Paul Gilroy describes the suppression of blackness achievement and contribution to the modern as "cultural insiderism." Paul Gilroy used the term "cultural insiderism" to describe the conditions in which people distinguish themselves from others with an absolute sense of difference. e.g. sense of ethnic difference.

In modern times, the United States has been home to a thriving African diaspora that has made significant cultural, scientific and civic contributions. More than 350 million people are identified as part of the African Diaspora living outside of the African continent worldwide. That is more people than the entire population of the U.S. According to the World Atlas, "The United States has an African Diaspora population of over 46.4 million people, about 13.6% of the entire country's population." This includes people born in Africa as well as those of African descent born in the United States. And as the population of Africa grows, this number will only increase. They are getting into politics, teaching, practising medicine and representing citizens in court, a vital part of the US economy.

Many readers of his book might already be aware of how George Washington Carver invented over 300 products made from peanuts: flour, paste, insulation, paper, wallboard, wood stains, soap, shaving cream and skin lotion. Some might also be familiar with the story of Sarah Breedlove, aka Madam C. J. Walker, the inventor of beauty products and the first woman to become a self-made millionaire in America. And through the Academy Award-nominated film, *Hidden Figures*, you may be familiar with the fantastic contributions of Katherine Johnson, Dorothy Vaughan, and Mary Jackson to advancing NASA's missions.

But you may not be aware that many of the products we use daily were created by black people. Here are a few of those achievements:

Inventor and engineer Lewis Latimer invented the carbon filament, a vital component of the light bulb used by Thomas Edison. He designed the early air conditioning unit. So the following summer, when you are escaping a hot day inside your cool house or car, don't forget to thank Lewis Latimer.

Dr. Shirley Jackson was the first African-American woman to earn a doctorate in nuclear physics at MIT. Her experiments with theoretical physics paved the way for numerous developments in the telecommunication space, including the touch-tone telephone, the portable fax, caller ID, call waiting, and the fibre-optic cable.

Marie Van Brittan Brown, a black nurse, invented the first home security system. Her patent laid the groundwork for the modern closed-circuit television system that is widely used for surveillance, home security systems, crime prevention, and traffic monitoring.

Otis Boykin's improved the circuit to heart pacemakers after losing his mother to heart failure. He is famed for developing IBM computers, a burglar-proof cash register, chemical air filters, and an electronic resistor for controlling missiles and other devices.

Lonnie Johnson, invented the most famous water gun and worked on the Johnson Thermoelectric Energy Converter (JTEC), which converts heat directly into electricity.

Charles Drew was a physician, surgeon, and medical research-er who developed the first large-scale blood banks and blood plasma programs.

Marian Croak holds over 135 patents, primarily in voice-over-Internet protocol (VoIP).

Frederick McKinley Jones developed the automatic refriger-ation equipment used in long-haul trucks transporting perish-ables in the late 1940s,

Alice H. Parker patented the central heating furnace design in December 1919 and used natural gas for the first time to keep homes warm and toasty.

Lisa Gelobter was integrally involved with the advent of Shockwave, a technology that formed the beginning of web animation and online video.

Philip Emeagwali, a Nigerian America, also known as "The Bill Gates of Africa." In 1989, using some ideas he learned from the bees, he used 65,000 processes to invent the world's first massively parallel processing supercomputer — able to perform 3.1 billion calculations per second.

Jesse Ernest Wilkins, Jr. perfected lens design for microscopes and ophthalmologic uses. He developed mathematical models to explain gamma radiation.

Garrett Morgan first created the "safety hood" to help firefighters and the world's first effective gas mask. He also adds a third position, Yellow, to the traffic signal, reducing automobile accidents.

Sarah Boone in 1892 — Improved Ironing Board,

James E. West in 1964 Co-Invented Electret Microphone

Ngozi Okonjo-Iweala , Nigerian American economist, is the seventh director-general of the World Trade Organization.

Ethiopian American **Gebisa Ejeta** won the World Food Prize in 2009 for his research on making sorghum resilient to drought, extreme weather and diseases.

Three Nigerian-Americans, Esther Agbaje, Oye Owolewa, and Nnamdi Chukwuocha, won their electoral bids in 2020.

Tetteh Kwasi was a Ghanaian blacksmith who used his local knowledge of the terrain and climate to establish a cocoa plantation in Ghana in the 19th century. This was all the European scientists and botanist experts had tried for over 100 years to cultivate cocoa plantations in Ghana unsuccessfully. Ghana's cocoa sector also employs about 2 million people and constitutes a large portion of Ghana's GDP. It also brought billions of dollars to West African countries over the last 100 years.

Today 1.7 million people in the United States are descended from voluntary immigrants from sub-Saharan Africa, most of whom arrived in the late twentieth century. African immigrants represent 6 per cent of all immigrants to the United States and almost 5 per cent of the African-American community nation-wide. About 57 per cent immigrated between 1990 and 2000. [99] Immigrants born in Africa constitute 1.6 per cent of the black population. People of the African immigrant diaspora are the most educated population group in the United States—50 per cent have bachelor's or advanced degrees, compared to 23 per cent of native-born Americans.

Africa is an essential long-term strategic partner for the United States of America and Europe because it's home to more than 1.4 billion people, making it the world's second-most popu-lous continent after Asia. Africa is also an important source of raw materials essential to the western world economy. The continent has an estimated $24 trillion in natural resources, including oil, gas, gold, diamonds, platinum and other min-erals. In addition, Africa is a key partner in the global fight against terrorism.

This page intentionally left blank

10. IS SUBSTANCE MISUSE TO BLAME FOR AFRICAN UNDERDEVELOPMENT?

One of the unfounded stereotypes that are used to explain Africa's underdevelopment was black proneness to drugs and alcohol abuse than other societies. They then refer to drug use among blacks in the United States which shows that illicit drug use is higher among African Americans (13.7%) than Caucasians (12%) and Hispanics (9.7%).

However, an objective look at the UN Office on Drugs and Crime data does not support this assumption. According to the report, the top per capita consumers of cocaine, cannabis, alcohol and cigarettes worldwide are all in Europe and the US, not Africa.

In this section, we will consider the different nations' misuse of substances such as cocaine, alcohol, cannabis and tobacco consumption from the United Nations Office on Drugs and Crime website's recent statistics.

Cocaine

The United Nations Office on Drugs and Crime website's recent statistics was based on data collected for many years till 2014.

According to the figures, the UK is among the world's highest consumers of cocaine, with a recorded number of 2.25 %. Other major cocaine-consuming countries in the top ten include the

United States, Spain, Australia and Netherlands, along with a few South American countries such as Chile and Uruguay.

A surprising fact is that, while Columbia is a significant producer and distributor of cocaine, only 0.7% of her citizens use cocaine are only 0.7 %. Columbia stands in 34th place out of 115 countries and regions with high cocaine users, and African and Middle Eastern countries have the lowest cocaine consumption rates.

Alcohol

According to data by the World Health Organization that records the amount of pure alcohol citizens aged 15 and above consume per year. Russia was among the top alcohol consumers worldwide. They each drink over 15 litres of pure alcohol annually, which is almost equivalent to 155 bottles of wine or 1500 shots of vodka. However, Belarus is the country with the most recorded alcohol consumption worldwide, consuming about 17.5 litres annually.

The ten biggest substance misuse-consuming countries

	Cocaine	Alcohol	Cannabis	Cigarettes
1	Albania	Belarus	Iceland	Andorra
2	Scotland	Moldova	The United States	Luxembourg
3	The United States	Lithuania	Nigeria	Belarus
4	England & Wales	Russia	Canada	Macedonia
5	Spain	Romania	Chile	Albania
6	Australia	Ukraine	France	Belgium
7	Uruguay	Andorra	New Zealand	Czech Republic
8	Chile	Hungary	Bermuda	Jordan
9	Netherlands	Czech Republic	Australia	Russia
10	Ireland	Slovakia	Zambia	Syria

Cannabis

When guessing which country has the highest number of users of cannabis, one would think of Jamaica, the famous marijuana coffee shops of the Netherlands or Portugal. However, according to the United Nations Office on Drugs and Crime (UNODC), Iceland is the biggest cannabis-consuming nation, followed by the United States.

Tobacco

Knowing that tobacco causes the death of more than half of the regular smokers and realising that currently, 1.1 billion people (both men and women) aare regular smokers, the issue becomes quite serious and alarming. In 2016 alone, 884,000 died from secondhand smoke, while more than 6 million individuals died annually from first-hand smoking.

Eastern European countries mostly lead the ranks in the rate of smoking. According to the records compiled by Tobacco Atlas, Andorra takes the lead with an estimate of 6,398 legally sold cigarettes (both machine-made and roll-your-own) which are consumed per person annually. Luxemburg occupies second place on the list of most smoking nations, and Belarus, the country that occupies first place worldwide in alcohol consumption, comes third in cigarette consumption. On the other hand, the Tobacco Atlas list of the least smoking countries in the world records is African nations, and Nigeria is the only African country with the first ten in substance misuse.

Based on the facts and figures, it is clear that Africans do not take more drugs than people from other continents. The fact that the media and some schools project this stereotype doesn't mean that those are truthful realities.

This page intentionally left blank

11. THE IMPACT OF SLAVERY ON AFRICA

"The last four or five hundred years of European contact with Africa produced a body of literature that presented Africa in a very bad light and Africans in very lurid terms. The reason for this had to do with the need to justify the slave trade and slavery"

—*Chinua Achebe*

One of the greatest assaults on the development of Africa was the trans-Atlantic slave trade by the Europeans. However, before the trans-Atlantic slave trade, the Continent had suffered for centuries from the trans-Sahara slave trade by the Arabs. The trans-Sahara slave trade, with its destruction of the history and identity of the African man, only set Africa up for a more brutal and institutionalized slave trade venture by the Europeans. The trans-Atlantic slave trade provided Europe with all the cheap but skilled agricultural labour needed to become far more developed and richer than any other continent on earth. So, as Europe grew, Africa was being robbed of the very agile population it needed to build its Agricultural system.

Slavery is one of human history's most terrible crimes and injustices — the treatment of human beings as property and deprivation of personal rights.

An enslaved person is someone who is:

- Forced to work through mental intimidation or physical threat, e.g. beating and torture.

- Physically constrained or has restrictions placed on their freedom of movement.

- De-humanised and treated as means of production.

- Traded, bought, and sold as 'property'.

Slavery occurred in almost every ancient civilization, including ancient Egypt, ancient China, Persia, ancient Greece, the Roman Empire, the Arab Islamic Caliphate, and Sultanate. Typically, ancient slavery consists of a mixture of debt-slavery, punishment for crime, prisoners of war, child abandonment, and children born to slaves. This form of slavery, however, pales in comparison to what transpired in Africa from the 7th century to the 20th century.

Two major slave trades took place in Africa:

1. The trans-Saharan slave trade
2. The trans-Atlantic slave trade:

The trans-saharan slave trade

Chouki El Hamel wrote the following: *"With the advance of Islam into Africa, slave raiding in western sub-Saharan Africa increased and became even more common when the supply of slaves acquired either through purchase or as captives of war in the Iberian Peninsula and the Black Sea began to dwindle once the jihads, or holy wars, fought by Islamic states in the region died down. The decrease in the European supply of Slavs to the Muslims of the southern regions was also the result of an economic imperative."* — an official document from the British Consulate in Mogador dated April 12, 1876, by Consul R. Drummond Hay, stated:

The trans-Saharan slave trade started when the Arabs began to invade Africa in large numbers from 749 CE and settled in Alexandria, Egypt. The Arabs were mistakenly perceived by Africans as cousins and were welcomed as saviours from the oppressive rule of Byzantium (Graeco-Roman or Christian domination). The Arabs did not initially force their religion on the African Egyptians, but the Qur'an could not be translated into local languages like the Bible. As a result, literacy in Arabic soon spread and was assisted by intermarriages, and Islam soon became the land's religion.

Arab Slavery
Source superstock.com

After the Arabs had conquered Egypt and shortly after Muhammad's death, they began demanding Nubian slaves from the south, which continued for 600 years. Dominated African kingdoms were forced to regularly send tributes of enslaved people to the Arab ruler in Cairo. From as early as the 6th century CE, Arabs had developed slavery supply networks out of Africa, from the Sahara to the Red Sea and from Ethiopia, Somalia and East Africa, to feed demands for slaves all over the Arab world and the Indian Ocean region.

Between 650 CE and 1905 CE, over 10,000,000 African slaves were delivered through the Trans-Sahara route alone to the Arab world, and millions died en route. Enslaved African women were sold to households as sex labour, and offspring from the illicit encounters were primarily destroyed. Most of the Zanjs (Black) male slaves were transported to Lower Iraq. The enslaved African men were castrated and used as servants to do the meanest and hardest work at the Sahara salt deposits all over the Arab world.

With the death of Askia Muhammad, the Emperor of Songhai, in 1528 CE, Songhai Empire started falling apart. Ahmad al-Mansur, the Emperor of Morocco, saw this as an opportunity to conquer Western Sudan after his Spanish humiliation. In 1591 CE, he sent an army of some four thousand musketeers under the leadership of a Spanish mercenary officer called Judar Pasha. The war led to the destruction of African intellectual and material contributions of African scholars and the first universities in the world in Timbuktu, Mali, from human history.

The mid-18th century saw the growth of Islamic Tariqa and intolerance of tradition or other religions, cultures or customs. Usman Dan Fodio of Sokoto (Northern Nigeria) started out as a reformer and became the ruler of large tracts of land and people. When the Yoruba leaders in western Nigeria were fighting for supremacy in the 1820s because of the breakdown of the Great Oyo kingdom in West Africa, jihad leaders were invited from Northern Nigeria to intervene. However, the jihadist grabbed the leadership of northern Yoruba land instead. Their advance southwards, "to dip the Koran into the sea," as they called it, was only stopped after a hard fight at the edge of the forest into southern Yoruba land.

The chaos and devastation that followed the invasions finally set up Africa for the intense European slave trade. This trade-in African slaves, begun by the Arabs, went on uninterrupted from the 6th century CE to the 15th century CE, softening Africa militarily, culturally, economically, socially and politically, for the joint European and Arab onslaught on African people and economy, from the 15th century CE.

The Trans-Atlantic Slave Trade

The Trans-Atlantic Slave trade is the most infamous case of human trafficking in human history. The Trans-Atlantic Slave Trade stands out because of its global scale. At least 12 million Africans were taken from their homes and shipped across the Atlantic to the Americas between 1532 and 1832. They were forced to work till they died for landowners who 'owned' them.

The transatlantic slave trade started when the Portuguese used their economic and strategic advantages to navigate around west Africa to the Cape of Good Hope, South Africa, in 1495. After reaching the Indian Ocean, the Portuguese started kidnapping people from the west coast of Africa and took them as a slave to Portugal. So that by the middle of the 16th century, more than 10% of Lisbon's population were of African descent.

The Atlantic Slave Trade expanded to America for economic reasons. Many factors exacerbated the demand for African slaves following the European discovery of the size of the wealth of America:

1. The Europeans that travelled to America were too few and were not physically strong enough to handle the pressure of farming in tropical weather with basic farming tools.

2. The European exploration of America brought with it the introduction of foreign and deadly diseases to the native populations of America (the Red Indians). As many as 80% of Native Americans died from diseases brought by the Europeans.

3. The Indians of America remaining after the epidemy were not used to farming intensively. Most of the captured native India ran away or disappeared from the plantations as they knew the terrain well.

4. The Europeans decided to turn to Africa for cheap labour to set up a colony. The nearest Continent had a strong and healthy population and a well-established agriculture system that only required basic tools. The Africans were also a disciplined labour force and were able to work in the mosquito-infested plantation.

Europeans started to promote slavery among kingdoms in Africa by offering guns, alcohol, and manufactured goods to already established Arab slavers and African tribal leaders in return for abducting people to be traded as slaves. Selling slaves to European companies also allowed the tribal leaders to build up their kingdoms and set them apart from their rivals.

The slave trade was later backed by international trade between Africa and Europe. The international trade law created by the Europeans laid the foundation for the role to be played by the African economy within the global trading system. Today, this unequal relationship still exists between Africa and developed countries. The first part of the law was that Africa became a guaranteed market for goods produced in Europe, such as cloth, hard cash (cowries), iron bars, guns, gun powder, textiles, pottery, glassware, and beads, ironmongery, horses and brandy. Secondly, the law also recognised African people as transportable merchandise (slaves). That means if an African slave was thrown overboard at sea, the slave ship could claim compensation from the insurers. A 2014 estimate based on the slave voyages database suggests the number of slaves transported across the Atlantic was over 12.5 million and about 77 percent of these slaves (10.1million) were from the countries of Togo, Benin, Nigeria, the Democratic Republic of Congo, and Angola, and the Gold Coast (Ghana). However, this figure only represents the number of African slaves that landed alive in the Americas, the Atlantic islands, and Europe. Historians believe another 8 million slaves were thrown aboard during the Atlantic crossing or Middle Passage.

The author of "The Slave Trade", Patrick Manning estimates that about 1.5 million died on board ships (others have estimated ship deaths at 2.2 million), and 4 million died inside Africa during the raid, the capture and in transit from the interior to the coast. Slaves often travelled for many miles on foot in coffles — lines of captives shackled or bound together. Numerous deaths of slaves also took place, especially among the young, during their imprisonment at the Fort. According to Manning (1990), Africa's population was drastically reduced to 50% of its potential population growth due to slavery by the nineteenth century.

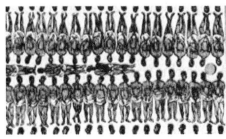 

Transatlantic slavery.jpg 1 and 2
Source .fastcompany.com

AFRICA'S POPULATION STAGNATES DURING
THE TRANSATLANTIC SLAVE TRADE

	1600	1700	1800
Europe	111	125	203
Asia	339	436	635
Africa	**114**	**106**	**107**

(Population figures in the millions. World population by region)

The table above clearly revealed that during the entire period of the slave trade, Africa's population did not increase while the people of other continents were increasing. Africa was the only Continent that lost its population to slavery in this way. It was the greatest forced migration of a human population in history.

The loss of population due to slavery devastated the development of Africa. Those captured for slavery were young men and women and boys and girls in their prime. They were rooted from their place of origin without permission and were transported to the Caribbean, North and South America, Europe, and elsewhere for over 400 years. The slave trade also exaggerated the difference in ethnic fractionalisation between African ethnic groups, caused the breakdown of legal and political institutions, and made them unable to enforce good behaviour among citizens. Of all the evil that the slave trade caused to the African Continent, the greatest is weakening trust. Trust is a key foundation for economic prosperity.

Slavery in Africa over a long period created a culture of distrust, pervasive betrayal, an uncertain environment, violence, and warfare that had detrimental impacts on African societies' culture, social, and agricultural development. Slavery affected the Africans' psychology and social fabric, especially in terms of violence and trust to date.

The slave trade also increased the prevalence of polyga-my (i.e. the practice of men having multiple wives). During the trans-Sahara trade, primarily females were captured and shipped to the Arabs for the sex trade, the sex ratio being about two females to one man. This led to the abuse, degradation of and violence of women.

The main occupation of the African populace during this time was agriculture, which was very labour intensive. The massive loss of the African labour force to slavery was immense. This loss became more critical because those taken in slavery were composed mainly of able-bodied young men and young wom-en who were supposed to be on the farm. European slave buy-ers preferred slaves between the ages of 15 and 35, preferably in the early twenties; the sex ratio was about two men to one woman. Europeans often accepted younger African children, but rarely any older person. They usually shipped the healthi-est wherever possible, taking the trouble to get those who had already survived an attack of smallpox and were therefore im-mune from further attacks of that disease.

Removing so many youths from the population over many gen-erations (a long period of 400 years) resulted in a huge reduc-tion in the number of babies born because these demographics are of child-bearing age.

In addition, slavery prevented the remaining population from effectively engaging in agriculture. Violence in the form of raiding and kidnapping rather than regular warfare led to in-creased fear, uncertainty, and insecurity that deterred many farmers from going freely to farm out of fear of being kid-napped. Labour also moved away from agriculture to more lucrative but brutal and disruptive activities such as war, kidnapping or being intermediaries for European slave traders.

During the slave trade era, many civilian Africans developed a vigilant and fearful attitude toward any foreigner. With the heightened risk of slave raids by Arab or European slave traders in the Western and Central Africa, Arab slave traders in East Africa, and many civilian Africans switched to subsistence farming and foregoing long-term planning.

An example of the survival strategy is a saying in Yoruba, a western African language, about the residents of the city of Ibadan: *"Ko si omo Ibadan ti ko ni oko. Ti ija ba be, wan o sa lo, pada si oko"* It means "There is no resident of the city of Ibadan that does not have a farm or home village in the forest. When violent conflicts start, they escape and head back to their obscure villages." Therefore, trading and life in populated areas were conducted with a disaster plan that if surprise attacks happened at any point in time, residents would flee by all free roads and unused routes leading into town. Without understanding that the continent at this period was undergoing instability and war due to slavery and that the only strategy was survival, European observers automatically assumed that Africans could not plan long term.

12. HOW AFRICANS AIDED THE INDUSTRIAL AGE

"We have to be honest and acknowledge that a large part of the money in our banks comes precisely from the exploitation of the African Continent. .... without Africa, France would slide into the rank of a third world power"
— *Former French President Jacques Chirac*

The European industrial age is often celebrated as a critical moment in the development of modern civilisation. However, little or no recognition is given to Africa for its vital but sad role in making it so. The great fortune made by the Europeans between the 17th and 18th centuries was built upon the backs of enslaved Africans. Today's most significant financial institutions and some powerful corporations have their roots planted deep in the trans-Atlantic slave trade.

Unfortunately, the average African man is either unaware of this fact or has moved on too quick, not considering the impact of slavery to date. However, for Africa to become great and her economic system rivals Europe's giant systems, there is a need to go back to the past to learn. Knowledge is the power Africa needs today.

Slavery was central to the British Empire and led to investment capital flows and the establishment of a market for manufactured goods. Enslaved Africans purchased by British merchants in Africa were transported across the Atlantic through the notorious Middle Passage to plantations in the Americas. These slaves were put to work producing various crops, principally cotton and sugar, which were transported back to Britain for British consumers. Raw material from the sweat of the slaves in the Caribbean created huge political fortunes for both the British government and consumers. Slavery helped build the institutional abuse system that led to the Industrial Revolution.

During the 17th century, sugar was a delicacy in the UK that only the rich could afford. However, Sugar plantations planted in the Americas and worked on by slaves meant that sugar was produced in far greater quantity than ever before. The price of sugar went down, making it more affordable for everyone in the British Isles. This further increased British consumers' appetite for sugar. It was not only the British consumers that benefited from the sugar plantations; the British Treasury also gained immense wealth from the trade. Some have argued that the sugar trade and Africans laid the foundation of Britain's Empire. Far beyond just eating sugar, the money from sugar grown by the sweat of African slaves transformed British society, built the country's infrastructures, developed ports, built roads and bridges, and transformed towns and cities and the populace's lifestyles and eating habits. It also created new wealthy elites and contributed immensely to the country's wealth and foreign reserve that funded the expansion of the British empire.

Before 1750, wool was England's primary source of income. But the industry soon discovered that Eli Whitney cotton gin machine used for processing wool could process cotton better. British slave owners started planting huge cotton plantations in the Caribbean. Slavery provided the cheap labour needed to grow cotton. Cotton production led to the start of the textile industry. Unprocessed cotton from the Caribbean was sold cheaply as a raw material to Britain to serve the textile industry. Britain sold the finished goods to West Africa and its colonies to make more money. Monies made was then invested into the slave trade.

Apart from cotton, Britain benefitted from importing various unrefined goods such as, tobacco, coffee, cocoa, and sugar from her African colonies.

Key features of the industrial revolution included:

1. Slaves were made to produce raw materials in large quantities

2. Products were shipped to Britain made in factories instead of at home

3. Workers used machines instead of working by hand

4. The machines were driven by water or steam power

5. As a result, one worker could produce much more each day: e.g. a cotton spinner could spin 200 times as much in 1800 compared to 1700

6. Cotton became Britain's greatest export industry

Slave trade also ushered in massive growth within the ship-building industry. These newly built vessels formed the base from which Britain would expand her economic reach to the level attained during the Industrial Revolution. In 1700, Liverpool and Bristol were small towns. Glasgow's population was around 12 000. These three ports became important cities by 1800, largely due to trade in slaves or plantation-grown products.

The tax revenue from these factories was used to build infrastructures, such as roads, bridges, rail networks and the electricity now enjoyed by Britain. This increased manufacturing, exports and overall economic activity stimulated the banking sector. Loans became a popular means of acquiring extra capital (which was always needed) to expand and maximise industrial ventures. Many traders and merchants directly involved in the transatlantic slave trade invested heavily in the banking and finance sectors. Present-day institutions such as Barclays, Lloyd's, and the Bank of England were built upon the transatlantic slave trade profits. With the rapid increase in both the frequency and value of overseas trade, shipping insurance became an absolute necessity during this time. Merchants made their money from buying slaves, but they didn't receive this profit until after the voyage and after the slaves had been sold. A voyage could take six months or longer. In the meantime, merchants had to finance the voyage, paying for the ship and sailors. They also carried the risk that the ship might be lost at sea. This is how financial, commercial, legal and insurance institutions emerged to support the activities of the slave traders.

There are countless other examples of critical innovations and entrepreneurial efforts driven by profits made from the Slave Trade:

- The development of the Boulton and Watt steam engine (a driving force behind the Industrial Revolution) was financed by the William Deacon bank, which wealthy plantation owners established.

- Key investors in railway construction, such as Gladstone, Moss, and Geocoyne, owed a significant amount of their wealth to the slave trade.

- Leading ironmongers Anthony Bacon and Gilbert Franklin used profits accumulated from their direct involvement in the slave trade to expand their entrepreneurial ventures. They are responsible for building the iron-smelting capital of Victorian Britain, Merthyr Tydfil.

- The Welsh slate industry was founded by the owners of sizeable Jamaican plantations, notably Richard Pennant.

The second most enduring impact of slavery was the promotion of racist prejudice and ideology. No people can enslave another for centuries without coming out with a notion of superiority, especially when those peoples' colour and other physical traits are quite different. The Europeans did not enslave Africans for racist reasons but for economic reasons to exploit African agricultural labour-power. After slavery, racism was used to justify the domination of non-European peoples during slavery.

In August 1791, the colony's slave population took a stand against a horrific and oppressive institution under the heroic leadership of Toussaint L'Ouverture. Thousands of slaves rose up and murdered and executed white owners and planters. And this led to the Republic of Haiti in 1804.

In 1807, the British Parliament passed the Slave Trade Act, which outlawed the slave trade in the British Empire. After the British abolished slavery in their Western Hemisphere colonies, they took on board a more daunting task of patrolling the Atlantic off the coast of Africa to prevent slave ships of various nationalities from continuing to supply slaves illegally. They also intercept the shipments of slaves from East Africa through the Indian Ocean, the Red Sea and the Persian Gulf. The British's role in stopping international slavery was estimated at £4 million. The dogged persistence of the British eventually reduced the shipment of slaves across the Atlantic and the waters of the Islamic world. On the issue of abolition of slavery, it was essentially British against the world.

By the 19th century, all slave traders lost customers because slavery was becoming illegal worldwide. And this was a big problem for some African countries with an economy that relied heavily on exporting slaves and importing foreign goods from Europe. They had suddenly lost their main source of income. Africa had not built up any other industries because of the slave trade, and it did not have any other source of income with which it could trade with the outside world. Africans could no longer buy many of the goods and tools they relied on. And as a result, Africa's economy slowly collapsed in the 19th century. Also, at the end of slavery, many of the stereotypes about Africans had been fully formed. Africans were viewed as people with no history and no established government. This belief system only grew more popular, aided by the weakness of Africa post-slave era. And, with nothing to offer the outside world again, the outside world took little interest in Africa.

Finally, with Africa's economy in shambles and European industrialisation in full swing, Europe suddenly could transport vast amounts of heavy materials across oceans. Before, transporting heavy ores from Africa to Europe would not be profitable because the technology wasn't available yet to make it profitable. But steam technology meant trains, steamboats and factories that could transport and produce goods at a profit. In essence, slave trade had fully equipped Europe with all it needed to launch a new kind of exploitation on Africa, colonialism, one that would cripple even more a continent with a weak economic system.

In summary, the British economy was literally built off slave labour. It was the slave trade that caused the emergence and development of Britain's wider economy, its financial, commercial, legal and insurance institutions all emerged to support the activity of the slave trade. It is no coincidence that the time Britain became a prosperous nation between 1600 and 1700 coincided with the time of the Atlantic slave trade.

However, many young people are taught that the wealth and success attained by Britain from 1600 to 1800 are attributed to the ingenuity and hard work of the British rather than the exploitation of African slave labour. Omitting such vital information is wrong and a disservice to the next generation.

This page intentionally left blank

13. HOW THE COLONIALISATION OF AFRICA EXPANDED THE EUROPE'S INFLUENCE

"Evangelize the niggers so that they stay forever in submission to the white colonialists and never revolt against the restraints they are undergoing. Recite daily — 'happy are those who are weeping because the kingdom of God is for them.' Convert always the blacks by using the whip. Keep their women in nine months of submission to work freely for us. Force them to pay you in a sign of recognition — goats, chickens or eggs — every time you visit their villages. And make sure that niggers never become rich. Sing every day that the rich can't enter heaven. Make them pay tax each week at Sunday mass. Use the money supposed for the poor, to build flourishing business centers. Institute a confessional system, which allows you to be good detectives denouncing any black with a different consciousness, contrary to the decision-maker. Teach the niggers to forget their heroes and to adore only ours. Never present a chair to a black that comes to visit you. Don't give him more than one cigarette. Never invite him for dinner even if he gives you a chicken every time you arrive at his house."

—King Leopold II (Belgian)

During the early nineteen century, there were many tensions, decades-long wars, and rivalry between European countries. Colonization was a ploy used by European nations to distract themselves from battling each other in Europe. In 1871, the king of Belgium decided that Belgium should have a colony, looked at the world map, and noticed that Africa was weak and available.

King Leopold II of Belgium set up the International African Association in 1876 and sent explorers like Henry Morton and Henry Stanley to go and research inland Africa and open up the rainforest of Africa to the king's agents. Officially, this was supposed to be a kind of international philanthropic enterprise in which the "benevolent" king would shower African natives with the blessings of Christianity and steam engines. These explorers discovered that the continent had abundant natural resources, including Gold, Copper, Rubber, Palm Oil, Diamonds etc. The discovery brought lots of attention to the African continent. European countries began to rush to Africa to gain control of huge parts of land that would give them access to gold and riches. Soon other European nations joined, and almost all of Africa was colonized by European empires. Europe's imperialists used the Berlin Treaty of February 26, 1885, to divide Africa into "Portugal, British, German, Italian, Spanish, French, and Belgian Africa."

King Leopold II demanded that Africans living in the Congo Free State produce a specific amount of rubber and ivory to increase his personal wealth. If these demands were not met, punishments included death, taking family members hostage, amputation and even burning entire villages to the ground.

As a result, 10 million people were killed under the brutal rule of King Leopold II. The international response to the cruel treatment of Africans forced King Leopold II to make the Congo Free State a colony of Belgium. It was then known as the Belgian Congo until it gained its independence in 1960 and became the Democratic Republic of Congo.

Below are a few factors that made African colonialism possible:

Congo under Belgian
King Leopold II
Source HM Stanley's

Belgium colonisation
allthatsinteresting.com

The discovery of quinine: Before the division of Africa, Europeans established modest commercial ports along its beaches. They only did business near the shore because of malaria and other diseases. Barely one in ten European explorers to Africa survived malaria and yellow fever. Thus, Europe nicknamed interior Africa "White Man's Grave." However, the discovery of quinine as a malaria remedy made Europeans explore hinterland Africa further.

Innovation: The invention of the steam engine and iron-hulled boats allowed Europeans to explore the continent's interior waterways, discover minerals and export large goods from Africa inland to Europe.

Explorers, traders, and missionaries were all accomplices in the colonisation of Africa. Exploration, trade, and evangelising often shaded each other and were frequently entangled with military force and the establishment of colonial rule. Traders carried European technologies of warfare and production as well as goods, while missionaries often advocated European social organization, education, and religious beliefs. All these profoundly alter the traditional patterns of African society.

"When the missionaries arrived, the Africans had the land, and the missionaries had the Bible." They taught us how to pray with our eyes closed. When we opened them, they had the land, and we had the Bible".

—*Jomo Kenyatta, the founding father*
and first president of Kenya.

End of Slave Trade: Slavery ended in Europe, leaving a void that business people rushed to fill. So when explorers reported finding raw minerals on the continent, European business people saw another opportunity to exploit black people.

European colonists easily invaded and ruled Africa because of three primary reasons. First, the slave trade had weakened Africa's institutions and structure. The locals had lost their ethnic identities, faiths, and ways of life to missionaries and Arab overlords to the point that they couldn't recall their past.

Two, the Europeans' military advances and savagery undermined the Africans.

The third and most significant were the colonists' ideals. Africans were made to believe that colonialism was in their best interests. The British and French were more effective than other Europeans in persuading Africa of these philosophies. That's why both remained longer in Africa and still do.

Contrary to popular belief, European colonisation of Africa was not an easy task. The coloniser and the colonised never had a loving or subservient relationship. All colonisers used violence and force to conquer the Africans.

Italian versus Ethiopia

The greatest humiliation suffered by a European state in the quest for empire was the Italians in Ethiopia. In late nineteenth-century Europe, Europeans universally despised Africans as backward and uncivilised. Italy had already conquered the horn of Africa and concluded a treaty with Menelik II, the Emperor of Ethiopia, in 1889. Unfortunately, the treaty broke down due to language misinterpretation in Italian and Amharic. In 1894, the Italians began military action. 15,000 Italian troops advanced in three columns, but they soon became separated and lost because the Italians did not have proper maps. They were met by nearly 100,000 Ethiopian troops, raised under the feudal system, supplied with modern rifles, and aided by 42 Russian field guns specially adapted for mountain terrain. Ethiopian cavalry slaughtered over 7,000 Italian soldiers and took 3,000 prisoners. This led to the resignation of Italian Prime Minister Crispi and exposed Italy to universal ridicule.

German colonialism

Namibia was populated by nomadic livestock herders from the Herero and Nama tribes. European arrival threatened their nomads' livelihood by an epidemic of a lethal cattle illness, Rinderpest, imported by Europeans towards the end of the 1890s. In the early 1900s, the colonial government's quick land grab led to the assault on German farmers. This offended Kaiser Wilhelm II, who feared being humiliated as Italy had been in Ethiopia in 1896. He sent 14,000 German soldiers from Berlin with the mandate that 'Any Herero discovered within the German claimed boundary, with or without a rifle or livestock, shall be executed.' The Namibians caught in the crossfire were murdered or hung.

The Germans then captured the rest of the tribe, chiefly women and children, along with Nama tribal members, and imprisoned them in "concentration camps" (the first official German use of this term). Those that survived were skeletons. The camps also became research locations for anthropologist Eugen Fischer, who became a key 'racial hygienist' during the Third Reich. The conflict decreased the Herero population from 85,000 to 15,000, while up to half of 20,000 Nama were killed.

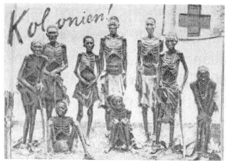 

Herero dies of starvation	British tortured Kenya
Source allthatsinteresting.com.	Source allthatsinteresting.com

Most African European colonies saw daily violence, including public beatings of Africans. The number of Africans publicly beaten in Cameroon climbed from 315 in 1900 to 4,800 in 1913.

British colonialism

The British empire was vast and varied, making generalisation impossible. In British settler colonies, like in German colonies, there was frequent and sometimes fatal violence, but by settlers rather than the colonial military. The British army devastated Benin and plundered thousands of artefacts. Royal Navy detachment bombed and machine-gunned Zanzibar's harbour, killing 500 people, to protest the sultan's nephew taking over without consulting the British consul.

When British immigrants first arrived in Kenya in 1902, they hoped to establish an agricultural colony that would assist fund other East African imperial initiatives. The British government then evicted individuals whose relatives had lived there for a thousand years, with or without compensation and put them in reserves. These reserves rapidly became overcrowded and overtaxed the marginal areas they were sited on. The Kikuyu, deprived of their land and rights, were pushed into rural ghettos and started mobilising. They went by Kenya Land and Freedom Army (KLFA) oath-takers but dubbed by British authorities as Mau Mau

In the summer of 1955, Winston Churchill ordered an unending campaign. The British erected a network of detention camps around the province for interrogation. One day in Nairobi, the British detained 130,000 males and deported another 170,000 women and children to the camps. The suspects were beaten to gather evidence. A British soldier's preferred interrogation tactic was to hold a subject upside down in a pail of water and force sand into his rectum. Men were raped with knives, snakes, and scorpions, while women were gang-raped or had their breasts damaged with pliers. Thousands of Kikuyu were malnourished, beaten, and tortured to death in concentration camps, and in some instances, most children died.

Francophone countries

Interestingly, France's hold on Africa remains strong among all the colonisers. African French (French: français africain) is a collective term for the 158 million Africans who speak French as a primary or second language. The French did not want to give up their African territories during and after independence and thought their colonies should not profit from their development efforts. To get their message across to other

French colonies, the French destroyed whatever they could in Guinea when the president of this African country tried to liberate itself from France. They set fire to food, livestock, houses, and literature. These heinous acts were meant to destabilise Guinea's new independence and staged coups against elected presidents of other colonies seeking independence.

As a result, other Francophone African nations were forced to sign cooperation pacts to maintain their links with France. Affaires franco-coloniales allowed France to develop a system of collaboration and conformity that lasted long after independence.

The obligations that France subjected some ex-French colonies under the colonial pact include:

- Paying for the infrastructure France built during colonisation — colonial tax.

- Keeping 50 per cent of their foreign reserves in the French Treasury — 14 African countries have been doing this for years. Interestingly, these countries can only access 15 per cent of their reserves each year. If they need more, they have to borrow it.

- France has the first right to purchase any natural resources discovered in their country.

- French companies have dibs on all government procurement bids

- Senior military officers are trained in France, so the personnel can be used to stage a coup.

- France has the right to deploy its military in the African countries

- African countries have to make French the official language and the education language.

- Using the French colonial currency.

- Former colonies have to send a reserve report to France.

- Ex-colonies cannot enter into military alliances with other countries without approval from France.

- Ex-colonies are required to join forces with France during war or global crises.

This agreement, which dates back to the 1960s, benefited French banks and the state but denied African nations income and progress. Since the monetary system was implemented, African governments have lost $500 billion, robbing Africans of wealth and development, and France would do everything to preserve it.

France controls the money supply, financial laws, banking operations, and budgetary and economic policies; Francophone nations have stayed impoverished. In Côte d'Ivoire, French companies own and control all the major utilities: water, electricity, telephone, transport, ports, and major banks.

This unchecked neo-colonial policy could not have succeeded if not for the African governing elites who relied on France's political, technical, military, and economic support. Any leader who disobeys France's will or tries to leave the French economic zone must deal with the consequences of political, financial, and military pressure. For instance, in January 1963, President Silvanus Olympia of Togo was assassinated three days before issuing a new currency. Other notable leaders include David Dacko, President of the Central African Republic; Thomas Isidore Nol Sankara, President of Burkina Faso; and Maka Modibo Keita, Prime Minister of Mali. All were assassinated or

overthrown in coups due to their quest for monetary independence. France has intervened militarily 40 times across Africa
since the 1960s.

Though the French monetary system is illegal, African countries cannot afford to sue. The world community is aware of
this deception but does nothing.

14. THE CONSEQUENCES OF THE COLONISATION OF AFRICAN COUNTRIES

British Prime Minister Lord Salisbury duly captured the arbitrariness of the partitioning exercise. He said:

> *"We have been engaged in drawing lines upon maps of a continent where no white man's feet have ever trod. We have been giving away to ourselves mountains and rivers and lakes, only hindered by the small impediment that we never knew exactly where the mountains and rivers and lakes were."*

Below are the few consequences of the partitioning of Africa by Europe.

Civil Wars

As a result of the partition and colonisation, in most African nations, a large portion of the population (approximately 40–45%) was placed together along national borders where there was no commonality. Some old adversaries were reunited. Europe drew the split for economic reasons, not because they understood or cared about any of these ethnic groups or where their borders began or ended. Some ethnic groups are split between two or more nations. For example, the Maasai were divided between Kenya (62%), Tanzania (38%) and Tanzania (62%), whereas the Anyi was split between Ghana (58%) and Ivory Coast (42%). The Malinke ethnic group has the highest index score, followed by the Ndembu (Angola, Zaire, and Zambia) and the Nuke (Angola, Namibia, Zambia, and Botswana).

Lumping together ethnic groups with long historical hatred led to above-average ethnic strife in Sub-Saharan Africa. To understand the implication of mixing ethnic groups arbitrarily, we only need to consider the Russia and Ukraine war and the fight over the Donbas region. Russia claimed the region is part of the Russian Federation because the people speak Russian. And as a result, war broke out in Europe after 70 years of peace.

The European partition has caused more war and warfare in Africa than the media made us understand. The frequency and severity of these disagreements have reduced motivation and made it difficult to adapt and develop institutions. According to an empirical study based on 43,000 documented disputes in Africa from 1997 to 2000, the ethnic map constructed by Europeans was highly detrimental to peace.

Creation of Landlocked Countries

Colonial boundaries also created numerous landlocked nations, 16 of the 55 African nations are landlocked, making them unproductive and difficult to trade. As a consequence, goods entering and leaving national borders cost more. Decolonization left huge nations with poorly positioned capitals. Most capitals were closer to the port as opposed to being central, making governing challenging

15. AFRICA AT INDEPENDENCE

In early 1950, Mr Harold McMillan, a British Prime Minister, called African Independence a long and overdue "wind of change" sweeping through colonial Anglophone and Francophone Africa.

Several factors led to the agitation for Independence by African Countries. More than 600,000 Black Africans fought for Britain in World War II, 200,000 Nigerians and 65,000 troops from Ghana. The African soldiers fought for Britain in East Africa, Burma, and the Gambia, promising that their service during the war would lead to the British government granting them independence. This reward was supported and encouraged by countries that were allies of Britain during World War Two, such as the USA and the Soviet Union. They realised that Europe's colonial projects were turning local conflicts (mainly between France, Britain and Germany) into world wars by compelling colonies to side with their colonial masters in armed conflicts. It was no longer tenable to the United States for Britain to claim that it was wrong for Germany to invade and rule Western and Eastern Europe, but suitable for Europe. The barbarity of the 20th century's world wars made it clear to the US that Europe was not having a civilising influence on Africa.

In the colonies, natives involved in protests were regularly imprisoned or murdered by colonial authorities to suppress democracy.

First independence speech by Dr. Nkrumah
Source allthatsinteresting.com

However, at the end of World War II, Ghana did not get its independence. Instead, soldiers returned to their country with a high unemployment level. On 28 February 1948, a group of unarmed former soldiers came together to protest peacefully. They asked the colonial governor for the payment they were promised to contribute to the war. The British officials stopped the protesters and fired openly into the crowd. Riots broke out immediately, and the people demanded that the British set up a new government led by Africans if they wanted the riots to stop.

By 1949, Nkrumah planned to use non-violent protests under the slogan 'Self Government Now!' to achieve independence in Ghana's immediate future. As Britain was involved in the Cold War, the British government worried that if they did not respond to the ongoing protests and allow a democratic election in Ghana, the leaders might ally with the communist Soviet Union to get the desired election. This would be a huge loss for Britain as they would lose an ally in Africa. In 1951, the British government agreed to hold national elections in Ghana. Nkrumah became the leader of Ghana. With this new position, he demanded independence again in 1956. Ghana became an independent nation of Ghana on 6 March 1957. Ghanaian Independence Day has been celebrated on 6 March every year since. After Ghana won its independence in 1957, there was a domino effect on the rest of the British colonies in Africa. Seventeen African nations gained independence. Several African colonies declared their independence from Britain in the 1960s.

As most countries began gaining their independence in Africa, the world watched in anticipation to see what would become of a free Africa. Unfortunately, things have not turned out as well as expected. Most African Nations plunged into civil wars, insecurity, Coup de tat, and economic and political instability. The abysmal failure of most African nations after independence remains a complex issue for most people. However, there are several factors to consider when deciphering why Africa has not done well post-independence in both leadership and economy.

INTERNAL FACTORS

- The colonial powers left an authoritarian legacy. Colonialism was not a democratic rule; it was an oppressive way of ruling that used brutality to keep the colonial subjects quiet. During this period, Africans had no say in how they were governed: the Colonial Office in Europe controlled all decisions. The first generation of African leaders inherited this kind of authoritarian control, not democracy, from European colonisation.

- Colonial Europeans also failed to prepare African governments for democratic leadership effectively. African leaders lacked the necessary skills to run the country.

- As mentioned earlier, African independence occurred during the Cold War after WWII. The Cold War was a period of geopolitical conflict between the US and the USSR and their respective allies, and the two superpowers' ideological and geopolitical rivalry fuelled the war. To escape the colonial system and the economic imperative (capitalism) that had held Africans down for generations, most new African leaders adopted the socialist philosophy. Leaders and countries assumed to be sympathetic to the USSR were severely punished economically by the west. The same is happening now with the Ukraine-Russia war, where the West (especially the US and France) is compelling African countries to support Ukraine.

- Finally, after slavery and colonialism, the new African leaders who had helped their nation gain independence were adored and idolised. This fuelled authoritarian impulses and stifled competitive, meaningful politics. The governing class used bribing, nepotism, and unlawful takeover of private property to reward political loyalty and gain followers' support. These "undermined governmental authority and harmed the country's growth potential.

EXTERNAL FACTORS

- Following the independence, local politics forced many African nations to accelerate development initiatives through considerable economic investment, infrastructure expansion, and growth stimulation. Most of this money was raised via borrowing, and credit was easy to get in the 1970s when agricultural commodities were cheap.

- As a result of the agricultural commodity price crash in the 80s, several African governments found themselves in considerable financial difficulty. These countries depended heavily on agricultural commodities for foreign exchange.

In a bid to manage the above crises, African leaders began to seek help from the IMF and World Bank. During this vulnerable moment, African ex-colonizers used their majority votes to demand from the World Bank and IMF to force African governments to open their market. These include selling only their unprocessed raw commodities to the west to gain cash, open their economies, and enable European firms to sell their goods to Africa with little restrictions. The international institution program led to an over-dependent on the importation of goods and the premature collapse of Africa's manufacturing industry, resulting in premature deindustrialization

The African debt issue was exacerbated by the African governments' mismanagement of the fund. The money was squandered on expensive and ineffective governmental operations, and the borrowed funds were mishandled. These dynamics have disastrously led Africa into heavy debt. Consequently, Sub-Saharan Africa's foreign debt surged from $238 billion in 2008 to $583 billion in 2018, ensuring a yearly capital transfer from Africa to industrialised nations. Most African governments have struggled with debt sustainability and have been unable to escape the financial trap, demanding debt restructuring and relief. Creditor governments and organisations have made many efforts in response to Africa's debt issue. However, without the right conditions for genuinely open international commerce, free of discrimination and double standards, African nations will remain poor and in debt.

MILITARY INTERVENTIONS

During colonialism, the African army played a vital role. For example, the British military believed in enlisting disgruntled people or minorities from a country. They believe soldiers recruited from these areas were mentally separated from people living in metropolitan areas. This dis-connection helped them be more ruthless when they were deployed to stop anti-colonial protests.

The Europeans also invested and prepared the elite of colonially educated Africans to carry out coups on their behalf. Future leaders were selected and trained in Colonial war colleges like the King's African Rifles, the French Free Army, and the Congolese Force Publique. These colleges produced military majors and generals who led most of the coups in Africa, thereby eroding political systems.

The years between 1960 and 1970 have generally been called the decade of coups' in Africa. Coup swept through the entire continent at an alarmingly high rate, and they leapt through national borders as if those boundaries did not exist anymore. By 1975, approximately half of the continent's states were led by military or civil-military governments.

16. THE FUTURE OF AFRICA

African Independence was a significant turning point in African history, even though it didn't lead to political stability and emancipation for all African countries. Africa's population is expected to grow by almost half by 2030, making it the world's youngest continent. The UN defines youth as 15–24 years old. By 2050, Africa will have the bulk of the world's youth. This rapid increase can yield a good demographic dividend as the population represents more opportunities for trade and income markets.

If well managed, demographic change will present significant opportunities for Sub-Saharan Africa. It will boost the working-age population's share and directly increase per capita income by increasing economic production and labour income per family. Along with this will be the growth in saving rates among working-age people, and savings will enable greater investment. The demographic gain will also encourage more women to enter the workforce, and when this occurs, both child mortality and fertility rate fall. Female labour involvement always increases growth and inclusion.

To build a modern, inclusive economy, policymakers in sub-Saharan Africa will need to get some basics right to create a solid foundation and steady economic transformation.

LET US GET THE BASICS RIGHT FIRST.

To build a modern, inclusive economy, policymakers in sub-Saharan Africa will need to get some few basics right.

Good Food

> *"It's important for our Nation to be able to grow foodstuffs to feed our people. Can you imagine a country that could not grow enough food to feed the people? It would be a nation subject to international pressure, and it would be a nation at risk. And so when we're talking about our national agriculture, we're really talking about a national security issue."*
> —*former United States President George W. Bush in 2001.*

Food self-sufficiency is the ability of domestic production to meet local consumption, particularly of staple food crops. The capacity of African farmers to produce and grow staple food crops within the continent, with minimum dependency on the international market, will ensure sufficient food is available to feed the local population.

Africa's ability to be food sufficient is ever more critical, especially now that the current war in Ukraine and Russia. This war, many miles away from Africa, is causing the cost of bread, grains and other foodstuffs to skyrocket to an all-time high. It is important to note that our Africans' ancestors have domesticated crops that would pave the road for future generations to live sufficiently depending on their agricultural products rather than spending billions on food. Money that could be spent on developing Africa's societies.

These activities will also encourage the development of small-medium enterprises (SMEs) that will add value to the raw food produced by farmers and create jobs(from farmers to chefs). Food self-sufficiency will save foreign exchange that can be used to purchase other agricultural commodities that cannot be produced locally. For example, focusing on cultivating sorghum will make Africa self-sufficient in food and provide levers to develop into a global net exporter rather than a net importer. A long-term strategy on food sufficiency will allow Africa to respond rapidly to countries undergoing climate disasters such as famine and war (e.g. civil war or Ukraine Russian war) within Africa and only get additional help from the outside world.

Adding value to agriculture

Local agricultural processing is vital to Africa's food. While African farmers put a lot of effort into their crops or livestock, they tend to get the least out of them in the market. Most foods are eaten fresh, and any leftovers are thrown away, so there hasn't been any urgency before to consume food efficiently, let alone preserve it. It is only through value addition that this trend can be reversed.

In addition, the increase in the middle class and the expanding population are pushing Africa's food import bill higher yearly. African agricultural imports have grown faster than agricultural exports and, by 2007, reached a record high of $47 billion, yielding a deficit of $22 billion. The value of agricultural exports of rice from Thailand alone is now greater than that of the whole of the African continent below the Sahara.

According to Mr. Adesina, *"agriculture is no longer a way of life for Africans; it is a business, a wealth-creating sector." Africa spends $35 billion annually importing food that it could produce* *by itself. It is estimated that Africa will spend another $110 billion importing food within the next five years.*

He continued, *"Africa has to add value to everything it produces and create wealth for herself. At present, Africa accounts for 75% of the global production of cocoa. Still, Africa gets only 2% of a $100 billion market for chocolates. While the price of cocoa is falling and cocoa farmers in Africa are losing billions of dollars, the price of chocolate remains the same and never goes down. So too is the price of cotton, and it keeps falling while the cost of textiles never goes down. The price of coffee beans also drops, but never the price of brewed coffee. Africa has to develop its agricultural value chains to add value to everything it produces. This would lead to a sustainable, solid rural sector.*

Value-added Agriculture is a worthwhile investment that can generate higher returns, allow penetration of a new potentially high-value market, extend the production season, create a brand identity and develop brand loyalty. Value-added agriculture generally focuses on production or manufacturing processes, marketing, or services that increase the value of primary agricultural produce, perhaps by increasing appeal to the consumer and the consumer's willingness to pay a premium over similar but undifferentiated products.

There are many constraints to value addition, first is a lack of resources, including refrigeration and cold storage, vehicles, and skilled personnel. Better infrastructure will assist in reducing trade costs and help African manufacturers integrate into global and regional value chains.

Post-harvest losses

The Food and Agriculture Organisation estimates that one-third of the food produced globally for human consumption is lost or wasted along the supply chain. This is about 1.3 billion metric tons of food that doesn't ever reach the consumer. This lost or wasted food is more than enough to feed 1.6 billion people yearly. In Africa, grain losses are even higher, estimated to be between 30 to 40% of the food produced, while fruit and vegetable losses are estimated to be 50% or more. Losses at the farm level are attributed to poor harvest practices and poor handling.

The loss of harvested maize and other food commodities is quantitative, i.e. losses constitute a physical reduction in the marketable volume, and qualitative losses refer to deterioration of nutritional quality, safety or grade.

Losses in storage are accelerated by late preparation of storage structures, late harvesting, poor storage facilities, storage bags with very low life span, and easily punctured bags by rats. Insects and other pests are a major threat in Africa to grain production and they are responsible for direct and indirect losses of grain on the farm and storage. Insects are responsible for 10-60% of grains' pre and postharvest losses. More than 470 million smallholder farmers suffer a decline of 15% income, while 25% of fresh water and 20% of farmland, not the manpower, is wasted on unconsumed food.

Government should train and sponsor Agricultural Field Officers that will go to rural areas and train and promote the traditional methods of preventing post-harvest loss.

Good water and sewage

Africa's health problems are not caused so much by diseases as by poverty. Over 80% of all illnesses in Africa are directly or indirectly associated with poor water supply and sanitation. It is estimated that safe drinking water and sanitation could cut infant mortality in half in much of Africa. Handwashing can cut diarrhoeal diseases dramatically, by 40% in the under-5 age group. There is a need for the government to be committed to digging or drilling wells, protecting natural water springs, or building water purification systems.

Good Health

Traditional African health services involve a centrally planned, "top-down" approach, favouring items such as healthy hospital beds, drugs, patients, and expensive equipment. The alternative to this is "primary health care" (PHC), which means getting health care out of hospitals, out of the hands of doctors, and into communities. PHC emphasizes education and the hardware of health (piped water, protected wells, sanitation systems, safe food storage) rather than the hardware of disease. For the price of one doctor's education, more than 60 community health workers could be trained and sent to rural communities where most health problems are.

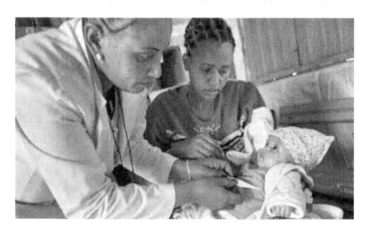

Education

According to UNICEF, the number of children in Africa who are in school has risen by 35 per cent in 2000 from 17 per cent in

2019. However,105 million primary and secondary school children were still out of school in Africa. One in three children does not complete primary school.

As the population increases, education becomes more important because the needs of people are rising. With rising needs comes rising productivity and a need for educated people to create productivity. Promoting an education system that is "fit for purpose" with a strong focus on entrepreneurship and technology is critical to optimising opportunities. Investments in education will help break intergenerational poverty cycles and aid socio-economic development. This leads to a qualified and employable workforce that meets the demands of the labour markets for skills and competencies.

Africa can learn from the examples of the economies of the four Asian Tigers. Studies showed that the economies of South Korea, Hong Kong, Singapore, and Taiwan maintained high growth rates and rapid industrialization between the early 1960s and 1990s. These territories focused on improving the education system at all levels; heavy emphasis was placed on ensuring that all children attended elementary and compulsory high school education. There is also a pressing need for more qualified teachers in schools. According to UNICEF, Africa needs 17 million additional teachers to achieve universal primary and secondary education by 2030.

Improve Energy supply and demand

Economic transformation in sub-Saharan Africa will require a significant increase in energy supply. Some 620 million people lack access to electricity. However, Sub-Saharan Africa has a few good things going for it on energy. For one, it has an enormously rich portfolio of clean energy assets: about 1,100 gigawatts (GW) of solar capacity, 350 GW of hydro, and 109

GW of wind. In addition, global technological progress has created the potential for developing countries to leapfrog to more energy-efficient processes and products not available to other countries as they developed decades ago. African universities should research and develop more affordable and effective solar panels so that Africa leapfrog directly to mobile phones, bypassing landline connections. Africa also needed to embrace renewable energy to leapfrog older power generation technologies while reducing the need to extend the national energy grid to remote villages. From an African perspective, renewable energy technologies, such as solar and wind power, have two powerful advantages: speed and decentralization. They can be rolled out much more quickly than fossil fuel-fired power plants, and they can operate both on grid and off grid.

The most stunning example of Africa's embrace of renewable energy is the Ouarzazate complex in Morocco, is the world's biggest solar facility and one of the cheapest concentrated solar power plants to be financed.

Managing the finances

Ensuring there is money to pay for civil servants, capital projects, and interest costs is important. A good government needs to be competent at revenue collection, picking the best services or projects to spend money on, and sourcing the best terms from capital providers — either domestic or foreign investors. Countries should try not to heap up unnecessary debt for the next generation for personal or short-term goals. Countries have to keep their lenders happy and also find ways to avoid excessive borrowing. Ideally, they should ensure there is no risk of default. Failure to manage loan creditors was the pretext for the invasion of Egypt by Britain and the invasion of Morocco by France, and now China in some African countries. African countries that fail to keep their level of borrowing sensibly are risking the independence of the country left to their children. They may be forced to sell national assets below market values to foreigners, which would be stupid. Politicians and civil servants who fail to manage the country's finances competently should not be tolerated.

Improved Security

Security is still a major challenge in Africa and needs to be improved. The drivers of conflict and violence include young populations, high unemployment, lack of equal opportunities, urbanisation, poverty, inequality, too many guns, and bad governance and corruption. With economic growth in Africa forecasted to grow at 5% per annum, there is an urgent need to ensure the growth raises people's living standards off the street and tackles extreme poverty and inequality across the continent.

Insecurity is debilitating to the economic development of many African countries. In the last 15 years, intrastate conflicts have outnumbered international conflicts, causing several million deaths, including civilians, annihilating basic public services and state institutions and generating extensive poverty among the populace.

According to Odeselu, cited in Shadare (2011), insecurity in Africa is like draining blood from a man. It drains the resources that could have been used to improve safety, including finances and time. Insecurity also increases the unit cost of doing business and the unit cost of production. An insecure environment impinges on development; it disenfranchises communities, contributes to poverty, distorts economies, creates instability and stunts political development.

Poverty and social injustice have long been the drivers of in-security in sub-Saharan Africa, and armed insurgencies and terrorist groups feed off this widespread frustration, especially among young people. With economic growth in Africa fore-casted to grow at 5% per annum, there is an urgent need to im-prove the country's infrastructure needs, e.g. roads, electricity, education, health, and other public services, etc., are spread across both the cities and the poorest rural areas. This would improve social cohesion and harmony in African societies and ensure the economic allure of Africa as an area of investment.

Good employment opportunities

A lack of graduate employment opportunities across the con-tinent has contributed to high informal employment levels, underemployment, and unemployment among university graduates. Many African nations have promoted formal skilled graduate employment through the Virtual African Higher Ed-ucation Observatory and the National Youth Service. There is a need to further improve youth employment through govern-ments, the private sector, civil society, etc. Governments can fund and promote private investment in skills development. For example, Uganda has offered grants for training and busi-ness materials to individuals seeking vocational training for small-scale businesses such as tailoring, mechanics, and hair-dressing. In other examples, governments subsidise appren-ticeship training costs or offer incentives to attract adolescents back to completing primary school.

Youth-friendly laws

The government must promote an enabling environment for youths and youth-friendly laws that promote human rights and youth rights. There is a need to support youth participation not only in political parties and in government and legislatives but also at local councils and at all levels of government to influence daily policy decisions at all levels. The lesson learned from the Arab Spring in North Africa and the ENDSARS protest in Nigeria is that the government should cautiously engage young people in politics because when they are frustrated and marginalized, they will have a sense of hopelessness and become challenging to deal with. The government's challenge is to move young people from the protest mindset to the political mindset. It is critical to harness the potential of the continent's youthful population and meet their expectations for education, opportunities, and jobs to create long-term security.

Managing diversity

The most complex civilizations and largest empires have always found a way to manage diversity either by incorporating the most talented people of different cultural backgrounds into public life peacefully. Countries which cannot be kept together peacefully should consider either devolution of powers to constituent nations or regions or a bloodless separation and avoid the atrocity that follows when a civil war breaks out.

Poorly educated populations will most likely be told the lie that other ethnic groups are responsible for state failures. The truth is both Christian, Muslim, and indigenous faith systems have produced impressive African civilizations in the past. Anyone who calls for a need to harm Christians, Muslims, or someone different from having faith-based leadership or ethnicity-based leadership rather than a meritocracy is lying. Uneducated Africans are less likely to spot lies because they do not possess facts or historical knowledge from the last 5,000 years. Facts are essential for spotting lies which this book has tried to relay.

Intra-African Tariff reduction

A major obstacle to intra-African trade is the tariff barrier. Firstly, it makes the process of trading extremely difficult. On top of that, it raises the price of imported goods and hikes transaction costs. To jump-start the continent's economic prospects, tariff reduction or total elimination of customs duties on imported goods from within the continent is necessary. This will create a more stable trade regime, continental market access, and a huge increase in the investment rate. The greatest opportunity for realizing Africa's growth potential is Africa's ability to trade and do business with itself.

Africa's growth must be based on more regional integration and freer trade. While the rest of the world is becoming increasingly broken and divided, it's time for Africa to figure out how to connect better its many different markets, which have long slowed growth and blocked trade.

Manage God-given resources sustainably

While Africa is blessed with abundant natural resources and land, poor management has damaged the environment, widened wealth inequality, and fuelled resentment and conflict. Increased population growth and climate change will put greater pressure on the continent. Africa will need to manage its water, mineral, and agricultural resources sustainably against internal and external enemies to reduce their negative impacts on security.

Africa's natural resources aren't limited to sunshine and other energy sources. It also possesses major reserves of minerals such as cobalt and platinum that are needed in fast-growing clean energy industries.

"Africa holds the key to global energy transitions, as it is the continent with the most important ingredients for producing critical technologies. For example, the Democratic Republic of the Congo accounts for two-thirds of the global production of cobalt, a vital element in batteries used for cars, mobile phones, and aeroplanes. South Africa produces 70% of the world's platinum, which is used in hydrogen fuel cells. As energy transitions accelerate, so will demand for those minerals. " Rising demand for the minerals that can support global energy transitions offers an opportunity for African mineral-rich countries, but failure to keep up with demand could not only hamper Africa's economic outcomes but also hold back the pace of global energy transitions. Responsible stewardship of these resources is vital, as is fair trade from the multinational companies that exploit those minerals. Robust regulatory and oversight mechanisms would be needed from the governments of these countries to ensure that revenues produce visible, positive results for local communities and minimise negative environmental impacts.

Fight corruption and bad governance

Bad governance and corruption undermine development and drive violence. There is a need to fight downstream consequences of corruption within Africa, including terror, drug trafficking, and organized crime. Equally important is the need for many developed countries to stop aiding, tolerating, and enabling corruption by their corporate and individual citizens.

The level of corruption in the African continent will decrease once African politicians realise they came into this world with nothing and will leave with nothing. For corruption to decrease, there is a need for self-satisfaction among both African politicians and citizens. If you are ruling as the president or governor, be satisfied with your monthly salary and do not participate in corrupt practices. If you are a civil servant or farmer, feel happy with your earnings and do not go into drug trafficking or other corrupt business because you want to be richer.

In addition, corruption gains ground without adequate transparency and accountability. Citizens pshould demand that the heads of every public and private establishment to give detailed accounts of their spending each year. This is the practice in China and the South East, and it has minimised corruption.

Finally, unemployment has made many people go mad. Creating jobs for citizens of Africa will go a long way towards minimising Africans' involvement in dirty businesses like drug and human trafficking.

Africa needs to utilise its diaspora's potential

Despite their economic contribution to the place of birth and adopted homes, African diasporas are sometimes not fully appreciated. In their adopted homes, they are referred to as 'immigrants', often eliciting a sense of unwelcomeness. They are often treated as foreigners irrespective of their years in the adopted country. In their original homes, they are perceived as a 'runaways' ready to pack and leave when the going gets tough at their place of birth.

However, these same diasporas are expected to contribute to their adoption through taxes, and the original homes do not refuse their remittances. The African diaspora is treated as resources that should be carefully tapped rather than embraced.

Throughout the sub-Saharan African countries, the contribution of remittances to GDP is growing. From 2004 to 2017, it grew from 0.93% to 7.47% in Ghana, from 12.31% to 18.70% in Liberia, from 2.59% to 5.85% in Nigeria, from 7.88% to 13.67%

in Senegal and in Egypt from 4.24% to 10.06%. This contribution is larger than the official development assistance from the West and more stable than private capital flows. It goes directly to the grassroots, where it is most needed.

While diasporas need to continue to remit money to their families every month, African leaders should look for a way and a system so that these diasporas achieving great things for the human race can return home to do the same. The potential gain from such exposure, experiences and education overseas should be brought back home encouragingly and deployed for the betterment of their homelands so that the next generation of Africans does not have to leave home to find better education elsewhere.

This page intentionally left blank

17. GLOSSARY AND TERMS

Aksum Empire — An empire located in the Horn of Africa that ruled from 100 CE to 940 CE. It was also called Axum.

Algorithm is an established, detailed, structured step-by-step instruction to solve a problem or carry out a task.

Apartheid — a policy of racial segregation practiced in South Africa;

Arabs — A people group from the Middle East who invaded and conquered North Africa in the 700s CE.

Berber — The native peoples of North Africa.

Boers — Dutch and French settlers in South Africa.

Caravan — A group of traders typically traveling across the desert using camels.

Cassava — an herb-like tropical plant with a long stock, found mostly underwater that yields a nutritious starch

Cholera — a disease marked by severe vomiting and dysentery that is often fatal; Water

Caste — A group or division of peoples that defines social order and rank.

Chariot — A two-wheeled vehicle that is drawn by horse(s). It was usually used in warfare in northern Africa.

Christianity- a religion based on the belief that Christ was the son of God and on his teachings;

Civilization — the culture and way of life of a people, nation or period regarded as a stage in the development of organized society

Climate — the average weather conditions of a place, a prevailing environment

Colony — a region or state established as the possession of a separate nation;

Continent — A large continuous expanse of land. Africa is one of the Earth's continents.

Cultural insiderism — is a condition in which people distinguish themselves from others with an absolute sense of difference to make themselves feel good, e.g. sense of ethnic difference.

Deforestation — the state of having been cleared of forests

Desertification — the process of becoming desert either from inappropriate land management or climate change

Developed country — a country with a highly organized economy;

Dialect — a regional variety of a language;

Drought — an extended and stressful spell of dry weather in a region;

Dynasty — a succession of rulers of the same family;

Earthquakes a shaking or trembling of a portion of the earth

Economic — related to the production, distribution and consumption of goods and services

Ecosystem — an ecological community together with its environment, functioning as a unit

Endangered — a plant or animal threatened with extinction;

Equator — an imaginary line that circles the earth, drawn equal distance from the north and south poles

Ethnic — of or relating to a sizable group of people sharing a common and distinctive racial, national, religious, linguistic, or cultural heritage,

Evolution — a gradual process in which something changes into a different and usually more complex or better form

Famine — an extreme scarcity of food

Founder effect — is the loss of genetic variation that occurs when a new population is established by a very small number of individuals from a larger population.

Fufu — The staple food of West Africa. It is made from yams.

Generation — a single stage in a family, clan or tribes history. Children, parents and grandparents represent three generations;

Grassland — land covered with long grass and low-growing herbs

Ghana Empire — Empire that ruled West Africa from 300 to 1100 CE.

Great Zimbabwe — Large city that ruled in Central Africa starting around 1200 CE.

Griot — A storyteller, musician, and historian in West Africa.

Hieroglyphics — A system of writing used by the Egyptians that used symbols and pictures.

HIV/AIDS — Human Immunodeficiency Virus / Acquired Immunodeficiency Syndrome; Health

Islam — A religion that believes in Allah and the teaching of the prophet Muhammad. It spread to North Africa in the 700s.

Ivory — A hard, white material formed from the tusks of animals such as elephants. It was used to make jewelry and other ornaments.

Kingdom — a country, city, or state whose head-of-state is a king or queen

Koran the sacred book of Islam wherein the revelations of Allah are revealed to Muhammad;

Kush — An ancient kingdom that ruled the land of the Sudan south of Egypt. It ruled from 1070 BCE to the 300s CE. It is also called Nubia.

Maghreb — The region of North Africa from Libya to Mauritania.

Malnutrition — poor nutrition because of an insufficient or poorly balanced diet or faulty digestion or utilization of foods;

Mediterranean — relates to the body of water that separates Africa, Europe and Asia or to the land and people around it;

Migrant — one who moves from one country to another or any person who moves for access to work, food or climate;

Millet — any of several small-seeded cereal and forage grasses cultivated for grain or hay;

Mali Empire — Empire that ruled West Africa from 1235 CE to 1600 CE. Was founded by King Sundiata.

Mansa Musa — Emperor of the Mali Empire who made a famous pilgrimage to Mecca in Saudi Arabia. He was one of the richest people in history.

Moors — The people of North Africa under Islam rule after 709 CE.

Muslim — A person who follows the religion of Islam.

Nomadic — a group of people who have no fixed residence but move from place to place

Nutrition — the processes by which a person takes in and utilizes food material to maintain health;

Nomads — People that travel from place to place to find food and pasture for their livestock

Pharaoh — The ruler or king of the Egyptians.

Population — the number of people in a designated area;

Post-colonial — of, relating to, or being the time following the establishment of independence in a colony;

Pyramid — A monumental structure with four sides that meet at a point at the top. The Egyptians and the Kushites built pyramids generally as tombs for their pharaohs.

Rainforest — A dense forest found in areas of heavy rainfall. Some of central and western Africa is rainforest.

Sahel — Region between the Sahara Desert and the savanna grasslands.

Sahara Desert — Large desert in North Africa between the Mediterranean Sea and Central/West Africa.

Savanna — grassland containing scattered trees

Slave trade — the capturing, transporting, buying, and selling of people as slaves;

Slave — a person held as property;

Sorghum — a tall tropical grass grown widely for its edible seeds or its sweet juice that yields syrup;

Songhai Empire — Empire that ruled in West Africa from 1464 to 1591.

Swahili — An ethnic group in East Africa. Also, the language spoken by many East African nations including Kenya and Uganda.

Tribe — a group of families, clans, or generations

Tsetse Fly — any of several sub-Saharan flies including those that transmit diseases, such as sleeping sickness, a serious illness marked by fever, lethargy, tremors, and weight loss;

Urban — relating to or characteristics of a city

Volcanic eruption — the explosion at an opening in the earths crust marked by molten rack and steam, usually appearing like a mountain from all the rock and ash produced;

18. REFERENCES

Abdeljalil Bouzouggar, Nick Barton, Marian Vanhaeren, Francesco d'Errico, Simon Collcutt, Tom Higham, Edward Hodge, Simon Parfitt, Edward Rhodes, Jean-Luc Schwenninger, Chris Stringer, Elaine Turner, Steven Ward, Abdelkrim Moutmir, and Abdelhamid Stambouli. (2007) *"82,000-year-old Shell beads From North Africa and implications for the origins of modern human behaviour"*. PNAS June 12, 104 (24) 9964-9969. *https://www.pnas.org/content/104/24/9964*

Ann Gibbons, (2017), *"New Gene Variants Reveal The Evolution Of Human Skin Colour"*. Www.sciencemag.com. retrieved Feb 28, 2022.)

Ariës, Marcel J. H.; Joosten, Hanneke; Wegdam, Harry H. J.; Van Der Geest, Sjaak (2007). *"Fracture treatment by bonesetters in central Ghana: patients explain their choices and experiences"*. Tropical Medicine & International Health. Wiley. 12 (4): 564–574. doi:10.1111/j.1365-3156.2007.01822.x. ISSN 1360-2276.

Bogdan, A. V., 1977. *"Tropical pasture and fodder plants"*. Longman

Chukwu G.O., M.C. Ikwelle (2000) *"Yam: threats to its sustainability in Nigeria"*, CGPRT Centre Newsletter, 17 (2000)

Cockburn, A. (1980), *"Mummies, Disease and Ancient Cultures"*. Cambridge: Cambridge University Press. ISBN 0-521-23020-9.

Cremaschi, M.; Di Lernia, S. (1999). "*Holocene Climactic Changes and Cultural Dynamics in the Libyan Sahara*". The African Archaeological Review. 16 (4): 211–238. doi:10.1023/A:1021609623737.

Cruciani F, Trombetta B, Sellitto D, Massaia A, Destro-Bisol G, Watson E, Beraud Colomb E, Dugoujon JM, Moral P, Scozzari R (July 2010). "*Human Y chromosome haplogroup R-V88: a paternal genetic record of early mid Holocene trans-Saharan connections and the spread of Chadic languages*". European Journal of Human Genetics. 18 (7): 800–7. doi:10.1038/ejhg.2009.231. PMC 2987365. PMID 20051990.

Dicks, D.R. 1971 "*Eratosthenes,*" in Complete Dictionary of Scientific Biography. New York: Charles Scribner's Sons,

Dorian Q. Fuller, Chris J. Stevens (2016) "*Sorghum Domestication and Diversification: A Current Archaeobotanical Perspective*".

Diringer, David (1982). "*The Book Before Printing: Ancient, Medieval and Oriental*". New York: Dover Publications. p. 252 ff. ISBN 0-486-24243-9.

Enwezor, Okwui (2010). "*Events of the Self: Portraiture and Social Identity: Contemporary African Photography from the Walther Collection*". Göttingen: Steidl. ISBN 978-3-86930-157-0.

Elias N. Saad, 1985 "*Social History of Timbuktu: The Role of Muslim Scholars and Notables 1400-1900*". Cambridge — London — New York 1985. ISBN-10: 9780521136303

Founder effect. (2022, September 5). In Wikipedia. https://en.wikipedia.org/wiki/Founder_effect

Fadhlaoui-Zid K, Haber M, Martínez-Cruz B, Zalloua P, Benammar Elgaaied A, Comas D (2013-11-27). "*Genome-wide and pa-*

ternal diversity reveal a recent origin of human populations in North Africa". PLOS ONE. 8 (11): e80293. Bibcode:2013PLoSO...880293F. doi:10.1371/journal.pone.0080293. PMC 3842387. PMID 24312208.

Glassonline.com — A Brief History Of Glass. Available from https://web.archive.org/web/20110415194738/, https://www.glassonline.com/infoserv/history.html. (accessed 11 may 2020)

Harley, George (1941). "Native African medicine with special reference to its practice in the Mano tribe of Liberia". Cambridge, Mass: Harvard University Press. p. 26. ISBN 978-0-674-18304-9. OCLC 598805544.

History of Europe. (2022, September 3). In Wikipedia. https://en.wikipedia.org/wiki/History_of_Europe

Hooke, C. (Director), & Mosely, G. (Producer) (2003). "Black Mummy of the Green Sahara" (Discovery Channel).

Holl, Augustin F. C. June 2020. "The Origins of African Metallurgies". Oxford Research Encyclopedias. 22 (4): 415–438. doi:10.1093/acrefore/9780190854584.013.63. ISBN 9780190854584

Huysecom E., Ozainne S., Raeli F., Ballouche A., Rasse M., Stokes S. 2004. Ounjougou (Mali): "A history of Holocene settlement at the southern edge of the Sahara". Antiquity 78, n° 301, 579-593

Hutchinson J.B., Silow R.A. & Stephens S.G. 1947 — "The Evolution of Gossypium and the Differentiation of the Cultivated Cottons". Oxford University Press, London, 160 p.

Ivor Thomas (1957) "Selections Illustrating the History of Greek Mathematics", tr., London: William Heinemann Ltd.; Cambridge, Massachusetts: Harvard University Press, 1957.

James J. Hoffmann (2020). *"The Development Of Glassmaking In The Ancient World"*. Available from *https://www.encyclopedia. com/science/encyclopedias-almanacs-transcripts-and-maps/development-glassmaking-ancient-world*. (accessed 11 May 2022)

Jablonski, Nina G. (2011). *"Why Human Skin Comes in Colors"*. AnthroNotes. Vol 32. retrieved 28/02/19.

Jideofor Patrick Adibe (2009), *"Who is an African? Identity, Citizenship and the Making of the Africa-Nation"*, Adonis & Abbey Publishers

John Hall (2012) *"Meet Mansa 1 Of Mali — the richest human being in all of history"*. Published by Independent.co.uk, 16 Oct *https://www.independent.co.uk/news/world/world-history/meet-mansa-musa-i-of-mali-the-richest-human-being-in-all-history-8213453.html*

Katherine Unger Baillie, (2014) "The Varying Skin Colours Of Africa: light, dark and all in between", Penn Today, retrieved Feb 28, 2022.

Keita SO (2008). *"Geography, selected Afro-Asiatic families, and Y chromosome lineage variation"*. In Bengtson JD (ed.). In Hot Pursuit of Language in Prehistory. Amsterdam, Philadelphia: John Benjamins Publishing. ISBN 978-90-272-3252-6.

Korieh C.J., (2007), *"Yam is king! But cassava is the mother of all crops: farming, culture, and identity in Igbo Agrarian economy Dialect"* Anthropol

Lancaster A (2009). *"Y Haplogroups, Archaeological Cultures and Language Families: a Review of the Multidisciplinary Comparisons using the case of E-M35"* (PDF). Journal of Genetic Genealogy. 5 (1).

Loci Associated With Skin Pigmentation Identified In African Populations. Www.sciencemag.com. Dec 15, 2017. retrieved Feb 28, 2022.

Mafundikwa, Saki. 2004. *"Afrikan alphabets: the story of writing in Afrika"*. West New York, NJ: Mark Batty. ISBN 0-9724240-6-7

Naima Mohamud. (2019) *"Is Mansa Musa the richest man who ever lived?"* Published by BBC News, 10 Mar *https://www.bbc.com/news/world-africa-47379458*

National Centre For Scientific Research also known as Centre National de La Recherche Scientifique(CNRS). *"Discovery Of The Oldest Adornments in The World"*. Published by EurekAlert!. 18th June, 2007. *https://www.eurekalert.org/pub_releases/2007-06/c-dot061807.php*

Oyebola, DD (1980). *"Yoruba traditional bonesetters: the practice of orthopaedics in a primitive setting in Nigeria"*. The Journal of trauma. 20 (4): 312–22. ISSN 0022-5282. PMID 7365837.

Plaster, C. A. (2011-09-28). *"Variation in Y chromosome, mitochondrial DNA and labels of identity on Ethiopia"* (Doctoral thesis). UCL (University College London).

Penelope J. Corfield, 2008 *"Making History, Making History"*, developed by the Institute of Historical Research

Patrick Darling (2015). *"Conservation Management of the Benin Earthworks of Southern Nigeria: A critical review of past and present action plans"*. In Korka, Elena (ed.). The Protection of Archaeological Heritage in Times of Economic Crisis. Cambridge Scholars Publishing. ISBN 9781443874113

Rogers, Alan R.; Iltis, David; Wooding, Stephen (2004). "Genetic Variation at the MC1R Locus and the Time since Loss of Human Body Hair". Current Anthropology. 45: 105–8.

Smith, C. Wayne; Cothren, J. Tom (1999). "Cotton: Origin, History, Technology, and Production". John Wiley & Sons. ISBN 978-0471180456.

Stride, G.T & C. Ifeka (1971), *"Peoples and Empires of West Africa: West Africa in History 1000–1800"*. Nelson,

The National Academies of Sciences, Engineering & Medicine. (1996). *"Lost Crops Of Africa"*. The National Academies Press.

Ucko P.J., G.W. Dimbleby (Eds.), (1969), "The domestication and exploitation of plants and animals", Gerald Duckworth and Co, London, United Kingdom

Van Der Meer, M. (1995). *"Ancient Agriculture in Libya: A Review of the Evidence"*. Acta Palaeobot. 35 (1): 85–98. hdl:2381/4671

Van Sertima, I. *"The Lost Sciences of Africa: An Overview."* Blacks in Science: Ancient and Modern. 7–26 (1983).

Winchell F, Stevens CJ, Murphy C et al (2017) *"Evidence for sorghum domestication in fourth millennium BC eastern Sudan"*: spikelet morphology from ceramic impressions of the Butana Group. Curr Anthropol 58

Woods, Michael, 2009 *"Seven wonders of Ancient Africa"*, p. 61. Lerner books,United Kingdom 2009. ISBN-10: 082257571X

Wodhouse, J. 1998. *"Iron in Africa: metal from nowhere"*. In G Connah (ed). Transformationsin Africa: Essays on Africa's later Past. London: Leicester University Press.

UNESCO General History of Africa Volume 2 Chapter 5

Yafa, Stephen (2004). *"Cotton: The Biography of a Revolutionary Fiber"*. Penguin (Non-Classics). ISBN 0-14-303722-6.

Zaslavsky, C. *"The Yoruba Number System."* Blacks in Science: Ancient and Modern. 110–127 (1983).

Zohary D, Hopf M, Weiss E (2012) *"Domestication of plants in the Old World"*. Oxford University Press, Oxford *https://www.edutopia.org/article/teaching-african-history-and-cultures-across-curriculum*

https://www.sciencedaily.com/releases/2007/06/070618091210.htm

https://en.wikipedia.org/wiki/History_of_mathematics#Prehistoric_mathematics

https://en.wikipedia.org/wiki/Ancient_Egyptian_medicine

https://thinkafrica.net/africas-inventions-algorithms/

https://thinkafrica.net/kola-nut-the-untold-african-story-behind-coke-and-pepsi/

https://thinkafrica.net/africa-2000-domesticated-foods/

https://thinkafrica.net/iron-technology/

https://thinkafrica.net/steel-in-africa/

https://thinkafrica.net/food-domestication-of-yam-in-5000-bc-west-africa/

https://thinkafrica.net/sorghum-more-healthy-than-wheat/

https://thinkafrica.net/walls-of-benin/

https://thinkafrica.net/the-kingdom-of-benin-1660-years-from-355-ad-to-present/

https://thinkafrica.net/kingdom-of-aksum/

https://thinkafrica.net/the-ashante-kingdom/

https://www.unodc.org/wdr2018/

https://www.unodc.org/unodc/en/data-and-analysis/statistics.html

https://www.afro.who.int/publications/tobacco-atlas-3rd-edition

Made in the USA
Middletown, DE
05 December 2022

17075434R00116